POPULAR PRINTS OF THE AMERICAS

POPULAR PRINTS OF THE AMERICAS

# POPULAR PRINTS
# OF THE AMERICAS

By A. HYATT MAYOR

CROWN PUBLISHERS, INC., NEW YORK

*Grateful acknowledgements is made to all museum authorities,*
*libraries and private owners who have kindly*
*provided photographs and given permission for reproduction.*

"Original Italian version© 1973 by Electa Editrice"

Library of Congress Catalog Card Number 73-82943
ISBN 0-517-50601-7
Prepared and produced by Electa Editrice
Published by Crown Publishers, Inc.
Published simultaneously in Canada by General Publishing Company, Ltd.
Copyright 1973 in all countries of the International
Copyright Union by A. Hyatt Mayor and Crown Publishers, Inc.
Printed in Italy by Fantonigrafica

# TABLE OF CONTENTS

## Printing Starts in Mexico

Conditions in the Americas have differed so much from those in Europe that the definition of popular European prints—images for peasants and other people with antiquated prejudices—rarely applies in the New World. A more generally valid definition of popular prints in the Western Hemisphere might be something like images intended for people who care nothing about art as such.

The great Italian, German, and French production of popular prints that began before 1500, and was in full swing by 1550, did not spread to Spain, Portugal, and England, whence most of the New World was settled. Even the French in Canada came from the coasts of Normandy and Brittany, far from the inland print centers of Lyons and Paris. The only early immigrants who brought with them a European tradition of peasant picturemaking were the Germans from around Heidelberg. In Pennsylvania they continued to repeat traditional European images (ill. 40), to print almanacs like those then being published in German towns (ill. 38), and to brighten their rooms with moral pictures (ill. 39). They made a specialty of certificates of baptism, and blessings for the home (ill. 41). These were printed with margins wide enough to make room for angels, birds, flowers, fruits, and other symbols of a farmer's prosperity and contentment.

New World printing began in Mexico, the pioneer in most of Latin-American cultural life. In 1533, only fourteen years after Cortez had landed, the Bishop of Mexico, Fray Juan de Zumárraga, asked the Council of the Indies in Seville to establish a press and a paper mill overseas. In 1539 Seville's leading printer, Juan Cromberger, sent to Mexico his associate Juan Pablos, who had been born in

Brescia as Giovanni Paoli. Cromberger contracted to supply Juan Pablos for ten years with paper, ink, type, wood blocks (*viñetas*), printing equipment, all gratis, as well as clothes at current prices. He exacted in return 80 percent of the gross receipts and the monopoly of exporting books to Mexico. Juan Pablos was to be the only printer permitted there, and he might not dispose of any of his type or wood blocks. He was to sign his books "en la ciudad de Mexico, en casa de Juan Cromberger," a pseudonymity that he usually managed to evade.

In 1543 he published the first surviving American book, an introduction to Christian doctrine for the Indians, written (with borrowings from Erasmus) and subsidized by Juan de Zumárraga, the sponsor who had established the press (ill. 43). The only decoration in this book is printed from cast-off woodblock scraps. Cromberger had used the topmost border in 1526, and another Sevillian printer, Domingo Robertis, had used the left-hand border in 1534. In the central Spanish block of about 1500, the cardinal's hat obviously once surmounted a coat of arms that was sawed out to make room for type after the cardinal had ceased to be important. Juan Pablos soon bettered himself with an elaborate border from London and other cuts that look as though they had come from Basel and North Italy. These new acquisitions seem so unworn and up-to-date in their style that they were probably not printed from original wood blocks but from the type-metal casts of blocks that circulated at international book fairs. The number of non-Spanish blocks in Juan Pablos's stock shows as clearly as anything how much the printers of Spain depended on the world outside.

The first printmaker known to have worked in the Americas came to Mexico in 1568. He was a

Frenchman, born in 1538 in a bishopric that the Mexican records call "Gen" (Rennes?). He ran away quite early from a school at "Moncucu" and tramped with other schoolboys over northern Spain until he was twelve or thirteen, when he settled in Valladolid. There, with his French name (whatever that was) hispanized as Juan Ortiz, he learned woodcutting and probably other crafts as well. When his restlessness drove him to Mexico at the age of thirty, he began his new life by cutting wood blocks for a maker of playing cards, and also supported himself by binding books, hammering silver trinkets, and making corrosive sublimate.

In 1569 he went to work as a woodcutter for Pedro Ocharte, the French son-in-law of Juan Pablos from whom he had inherited Mexico's first press. Then in February 1571, the Inquisition, newly established in Mexico and more severe than in Spain, imprisoned both Ortiz and Ocharte on charges of blasphemy. Ortiz was accused of blasphemous conversation and of propagating false doctrine in a verse printed at the bottom of a woodcut that he had copied from a Parisian print of the Virgin of the Rosary (ill. 45). The extensive records of the trial show that he had printed three hundred impressions on paper as well as some on yellow taffeta, and that Indians had been hired to stencil (*jaspear*) the colors at half a real per print. For two reals they had also trimmed some of the prints, which probably meant edging the sheets with some sort of a decorative border to simulate a frame when the print was fixed to a wall. (Mexicans were still edging prints with gilt lacework in the early 1800s.).

The Holy Office interrogated Ortiz repeatedly during his twenty-two months in prison, and finally twisted ropes around his legs and arms, racked him, and doused him with water to make him cough so that the pain would stab. After an hour and a half of torture, he had to swear secrecy to everything that had happened in prison, to abjure his errors in public with a wax candle in his hand, to pay two hundred gold pesos for court expenses, and to be banished forever from all Spanish domains. Since he could not earn the money before the yearly fleet set sail, he petitioned to be allowed to stay in Mexico until the next year's sailing. Once his fine was paid, he vanished into oblivion, but the minutes of his long trial still preserve his name, his story, and his only surviving print, sewn into the court stenographer's pages.

No one knows just when native-born Americans began to make prints, but by the late sixteen hundreds Mexican books began to be illustrated with copper engravings that certainly look homemade. Many of these engravings appeared in booklets celebrating the masses and catafalques that honored the death of Spanish monarchs with mortuary spectacles splendid enough to draw crowds into the immense cathedral (ills. 43 & 44). The cathedral faced on a square vaster than any then in Europe, for Mexico was by far the most imposing city in all the Americas. Curiously, Mexico illustrated more books of royal funerals than Spain itself, either to parade the lavishness of its loyalty to the mother country, or just to remind itself of ties with home.

*The Start in British America*

While Mexican Catholicism was sponsoring these engravings, the Puritans of the Massachusetts Bay Colony began to make the first prints in the English colonies. Since these Calvinists condemned vain image making as rigidly as any Hebrews, the earliest North American prints were maps and portraits of the divines who legislated for Boston and its neighborhood. The earliest known colonial printmaker was John Foster, who was born in Dorchester near Boston in 1648, and graduated in 1667 from Harvard in a class of seven students. After teaching school at home in Dorchester, he bought a press from the estate of a printer who had died late in 1674. Foster must already have been interested in the graphic arts, for, presumably in 1670, he had cut the portrait of the Dorchester neighbor who had baptized him, the Reverend Richard Mather (ill. 46).

This English-born founder of New England's leading family of theologians, whose "loud and clear voice" thundered sermons with "a deliberate vehemency," also helped to versify the so-called Bay Psalm Book of 1640, the first book printed in British America. Mather's death at the age of sixty-three in 1669 presumably occasioned the publication of his portrait. This woodcut evolved by some kind of awkward afterthought. Why was it cut on two blocks? Foster may have started with one block of the present proportions, and then had to substitute a different body for some reason or other. Or he may have cut the head first, and when it looked insufficient, added the body in a second block. These blocks joined together neatly when they were first printed with no white lines to indicate the sleeve, and no typographic caption "Mr. Richard Mather." Then, perhaps years later, the torso block received two nicks at the bottom where only one had been before and was probably damaged at the top edge

as well. Damaged or not, the top edge was planed down, widening it so that it no longer fitted against the head, and the robe was suggested by incising white lines. The typographic caption was added, probably for a large edition, since this is the state in which most impressions have survived. The botching of this odd stark icon shows the effort of an intellectual struggling with a mechanical craft.

Richard Mather had six sons, of whom four became ministers. The youngest son, Increase Mather, grew up to sway the Massachusetts Bay Colony by preaching and by writing some one hundred and thirty books and pamphlets, including one in his homemade approximation of Spanish. In 1689, while he was in London for four years of negotiations for the colony, his portrait was engraved there, showing him at the age of fifty. In 1701 this London portrait was copied in Boston as a frontispiece for a book that Increase Mather published when he was resigning from his twenty-year presidency of Harvard College (ill. 1). This is the first copperplate portrait and the first engraved book illustration in British America. But why did the Boston engraver Thomas Emmes copy a twelve-year-old print when

Increase Mather was at hand to draw from life? Did Mather so shrink from recording himself for posterity at the age of sixty-two that he had his earlier portrait copied in such a way as to make him look even younger than he had been in London? It is more likely that Thomas Emmes, of whom nothing further is known, was too clumsy to draw anything from life, even though he could make a stab at copying the lines of an engraving. After all, it takes a considerable experience to devise patterns for representing an object that you see before you, while it is much easier to copy lines already established.

*Morals for Little Protestants*

Since the theocratic democracy of the Massachusetts Bay Colony knew that it could perpetuate itself only by educating its congregation, it established the world's first universal and compulsory free schools in 1647. Like the German Lutherans in the 1530s, these New England Calvinists attracted children to learn Protestant doctrine by illustrating texts. About

2. Metal cuts in *New England Primer*, Salem, 1802. *New York, Metropolitan Museum of Art, gift of Grace Albee.*

3. Woodcut in *Instructive History of Miss Patty Proud*, Hudson, N. Y., 1821. *New York, Metropolitan Museum of Art, gift of Josephine Lansing Allen.*

a century after the opening of New England's free compulsory schools, there appeared a tiny schoolbook, the *New England Primer*, that helped children to memorize the alphabet through rough little cuts and jingles of pure Genevan gloom—"Xerxes the Great did dye / And so must thou and I." Edition after edition perpetuated these pictures, first in smudgy type-metal relief cuts (ill. 2), like the illustrations for English ballads and broadsides, and later in neater woodcuts. After about 1810 hundreds of booklets were published through evangelical and Sunday school societies to help parents through pretty woodcuts that set examples by showing children who brushed their hair, spoke quietly, handled teacups without breaking, and in general did not bother their elders (ills. 2, 3, 5).

*Engravings of the American Revolution*

Colonial American engraving began to catch up with engraving in Mexico after the century that elapsed

between almost all cultural beginnings in Mexico or Peru and those in what is now the United States. For the first time, the New World began to do something that fascinated the Old World, when the American Revolution threw Americans into the stream of history with actions worth recording in pictures. The earliest, and for long the most famous print of an American historical event, showed the so-called Boston Massacre on the night of March 5, 1770, when some panicky British soldiers fired into a crowd, killing five and wounding six more. This minor riot was inflated into one of the causes of the American Revolution by being publicized in the first notable American news picture (ill. 51). Sensational pictorial journalism thus began to bend the course of future events.

The original print was apparently designed and engraved by Henry Pelham, a portrait painter trained by his father, who had made the first American mezzotints. Henry Pelham may well have regretted launching such a lacerating attack on Britain, for the onset of the actual Revolution turned him into

# Earthquakes.

Tokens of GOD's Power and Wrath. The Di[...]
of the prefent World ; and the approaching C[...]
tion, when all Things fhall be burnt up : Wit[...]
Defcription of the drowning the old World, and Chrift's
coming to Judgment. Being a Warning to Sin[n]ers and
Comfort to the Children of GOD

Second Epiftle of Peter, iii. Chap. 10, & 11, Verfes. But the Day of the Lord will come as a Thief in the Night ; in the which the Heavens fhall pafs away with a great Noife, and the Elements fhall melt with fervent Heat, the Earth alfo and the Works that are therein fhall be burnt up. Ver. 11. Seeing then that all thefe Things fhall be diffolved, what Manner of Perfons ought ye to be in all holy Converfation and Godlinefs.

## THE SECOND EDITION.

INSPIRED JOB fpeaking of GOD,
    The high and holy One,
Declares he's wife in Heart, in Strength
    He mighty is alone.
Who doth remove the Mountains great,
    Tho' ftedfaftly they ftand,
And in his Anger overturns
    Them with his mighty Hand.
Who turns the Earth out of her Place,
    And makes the Pillars fhake,
And all its ftrong Supporters too
    To tremble bow and quake.
The holy Pfalmift, when employ'd
    In giving Thanks to GOD,
For great Salvations unto him
    He often did afford.
Proceeds to fpeak of his great Power,
    And what his GOD had done,
When he appear'd and wrought for him
    So great Salvation.
That then the Earth, the Earth did fhake,
    Ye and did tremble too,
Foundations then of Heaven were mov'd,
    GOD was provoked fo.
And when the Lord of Life did die
    Upon the curfed Tree,
The Rocks, tho' obdurate and hard
    Did break immediately.
The Earth did quake and fhake likewife,
    A Token of GOD's Wrath,
When Jews the Blood of his dear Son
    Did cruelly fhed forth.
Again the Lord did fhake the Earth,
    When CHRIST was in the Tomb,
When from the glorious heavenly World
    A glorious Angel came.
Behold there was at that fame Time
    An Earthquake ftrong and great,
Which made the Watchmen at the Tomb
    To tremble fhake and quake.
Again when Paul and Silas was
    Once into Prifon caft,
And cruelly the Keeper had
    In Stocks made their Feet faft.
Like the dear Children of the Lord,
    They to their Father fing,
They Praifes fing unto the Lord

Remember what vaft Agonies,
    Your Souls were in that Day,
Expecting every Moment would
    Confume you quite away.
But to return,---the mighty GOD
    Hath wife and holy Ends,
When to a wicked fecure World,
    Such fhaking Calls he fends.
Hereby we're loudly call'd upon
    Aloud for to prepare,
To meet the glorious Lord and Judge,
    Who quickly will appear ;
With's glorious Angels and his Saints,
    Behold the Lord will come,
And give to every Soul on Earth,
    Their final lafting Doom.
Before him fhall be gathered,
    All Nations far and near,
And by the Lord's moft juft command,
    Be forced to appear.
And then the Earth fhall fhake and quake,
    More than it e'er hath done,
When GOD the Lord fhall judge the World,
    By CHRIST his chofen One.
For ever fince the World began,
    GOD hath laid up in Store,
In Heaven and Earth and the great Deeps,
    Vaft Magazines of Power,
[...]
    His holy bleffed Will,
For Wind and Seas, and Earthquakes all,
    His juft Decree fulfill.
When Man had finn'd moft heinoufly,
    Before the World was drown'd,
The Lord commands his Storehoufes
    To open all around.
No fooner fpake the almighty GOD,
    Unto the bounded deep,
But over every Hill it ran,
    And every Mountain leapt.
To drown a bafe unthankful World,
    Who Mercy had abus'd,
The Grace and Patience of their GOD,
    Moft fhamefully mifus'd.
Oh how amazing was the Sight,
    On Mountains Tops to fee,
So many poor diftreffed Souls,

But Oh the Stupidnefs of Men !
    Who will no Counfel hear,
Tho' GOD repeats his Calls to them,
    By Earthquakes, Death, and War.
When Noah warn'd the ancient World
    Of the approaching Flood,
No doubt like harden'd Sinners they
    Defpifingly then ftood.
No doubt they tho't the ancient Saint
    Not worth their noticing,
'Till GOD in his juft Judgment did
    The awful Judgment bring.
And an't it now the very Cafe
    Of Sinners at this Day,
Who will not hear the mighty GOD,
    Nor what his Preachers fay.
Altho' the holy Lord hath faid,
    He'd come in flaming Fire,
And punifh a moft finful World,
    In his avenging Ire.
That all the Heav'ns fhall be in flames,
    The Elements likewife
With fervent Heat fhall melt away,
    To their awful Surprize.
What an amazing Sight it is,
    To fee Men quite fecure,
When in the Heav'ns fometimes we hear
    GOD's dreadful Thunders roar.
The Earth likewife before the Lord
    Doth fhake and tremble too,
And roar beneath the crying Sin
    Of fuch a wretched Crew.
That Men can't be prevail'd upon
    Tho' with our ftrong Defire,
To get prepar'd againft that Day
    When all the World on Fire
Shall burn and blaze about their Heads,
    And they no Shelter have,
No Rock to hide their guilty Heads,
    No nor no wat'ry Grave.
For Rocks will melt like Wax away
    Before the dreadful Heat,
And Earth and Sea and all will flame,
    In one confuming Heap.
The Earth beneath abounds with Stores
    Of Oils and Sulphurs too,
And Turfs and Coal, which all will flame,
    When GOD commands the Blow.

4. Metal cut, Boston, 1744. *New York Public Library.*

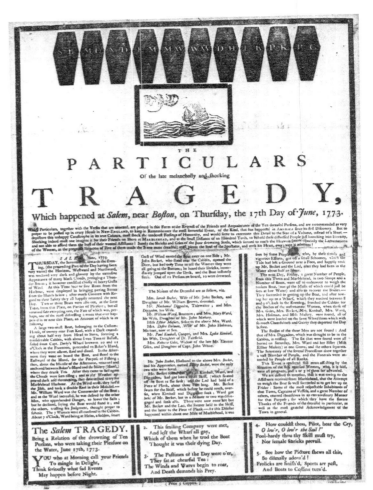

5. Relief metal engraving, Philadelphia, about 1812. *New York, Metropolitan Museum of Art.*

6. News broadside on the drowning of ten people. Woodcuts, Salem, Massachusetts, 1773. *New-York Historical Society.*

so ardent a loyalist that in 1776 he went to England for good to join his half brother, the painter John Singleton Copley. Only twenty-eight days after the fracas on March 5, Pelham advertised *The Fruits of Arbitrary Power* as "an original Print taken on the Spot." Alas, too late. One week before, on March 26, the market had quickly been glutted by the advertisement of a pirated copy of his engraving under the much more sensational title of "the late horrid Massacre." Pelham had been robbed of the reward of his enterprise by the aggressive silversmith, brass founder, and patriot, Paul Revere. Revere's copy is so accurate that he probably obtained an impression of Pelham's original quickly enough to be able to offset the still-fresh ink onto a copperplate by squeezing paper and blank metal together in a rolling press. The copyist's graver could then readily follow the offset lines. Revere's copy must have outsold all the many versions of the massacre, being still fairly

common. Prints of the massacre were so prevalent that the jurors who tried the British soldiers were warned by the judge not to be swayed by the dramatic license of "the prints exhibited in our houses." Revere's engraving is one of the earliest prints to survive in a contemporary frame and under clear glass, which had only recently become cheap enough to use for protecting prints hung on the wall. On April 1, only twenty-seven days after the massacre, Boston dispatched a fast packet to England with pamphlets and prints describing and showing the event. But the brisk market for prints of the massacre must have slackened as the greater events of the Revolution began to loom large, for five years later Revere shortened the worn copperplate and used the blank back to engrave bank notes of ten, twelve, and eighteen shillings for an issue in May 1775.

After this promise of rough-and-tumble native

10

subject matter for prints, the all-absorbing Revolution left little energy for art of any kind. Almost the only notable prints of contemporary events were a set of four engravings showing the progress of the battles of Lexington and Concord, the first exchanges of gunfire between British and American soldiers on April 19, 1775. The "shot heard round the world" promptly brought two young men from New Haven to see the battlefields for themselves and to record the event. These were the portrait painter Ralph Earl, then twenty-four, and Amos Doolittle, twenty-one, who had learned engraving in the course of his training as a silversmith, though he had never yet engraved a copperplate for printing. While the painter sketched the battlefield, the engraver posed for the big figures of British officers. Nearly eight months later the hopeful artists advertised their four prints in the New Haven newspaper of December 13, 1775, as being "neatly engraved on Copper, from original paintings taken on the spot. Price six shillings per set for the plain ones, or eight shillings colored" (ill. 52). Scratchy and tentative though they are, their factual reticence, their lack of sword waving manages to say clearly "I was there." But this very modest actuality that endears these prints to us now must have left contemporaries indifferent, for only one of the four original paintings has survived, and the engravings are rare.

It is curious how often an age fails to make prints of events which seem important to posterity. No one during the Revolution adequately engraved the signing of the Declaration of Independence or the British surrender at Yorktown. As soon as the war passed into history, people began to want portraits of George Washington (ill. 53). While he lived, Washington was forced to face some of the bitterest criticism that any American president has ever had to bear, but after his death in 1799 the Father of his Country became so deified that the Russian traveler, Paul Svinin, noticed in 1812/13 that every American living room had to have his portrait just as every Russian house had to have an icon.

## Making Paper Money Hard to Forge

The enormous cost of the Revolution accelerated the printing of paper money, which had begun in 1690 when the Massachusetts Bay Colony issued bank notes bearing the first known Colonial engraving—a tiny seal of the colony, too insignificant to reproduce here. The engraver was certainly John Coney, a prominent silversmith who held various municipal offices. It was logical to commission a silversmith to engrave currency because he was accustomed to using the graver, to handling precious metals, and to acting as an informal banker.

Although Coney seems to have been the first British American to engrave plates for printing, other silversmiths knew how to engrave and promptly forged his bank notes. Counterfeiters, who continued to plague the colony, frequently had to stand in the pillory (ill. 54). One of the forgers is said to have been a woman who made offsets of relief-printed bank notes by dampening them and ironing them with a hot iron against blank paper. It is easy to see how this could have been done by double offset with the simple designs on the quickly produced Revolutionary bank notes (ill. 57). These were the first large printings of decorative designs in the New World. The Revolutionary bank notes issued by the Continental Congress sank as rapidly as the French Revolutionary assignats or the German inflation money to something like one thousandth of their face value, a ruin that some Americans recall when they say that something "is not worth a Continental."

Bank notes were easy to forge the world over until 1806 when Jacob Perkins, an iron founder in Newburyport, Massachusetts, published a booklet describing his invention of a method for case hardening an engraved block of soft steel without damaging the engraving. He then passed a soft steel roller over the block with enough pressure to force the soft steel down into the grooves in the hardened block. Case-hardened in its turn, the roller repeated its design any number of times by pressing its ridges into a large printing plate of copper or steel (ill. 7). Perkins also combined gears and cams to engrave interplays of swirls too intricate to copy by hand, as can be seen in any dollar bill today. These innovations, America's main contribution to the technique of printmaking, enabled United States engravers to supply the world with bank notes, bond certificates, and postage stamps.

## Color Woodcuts and Early Manufacturing

In other kinds of printing, America followed the lead of Europe. About 1830 Boston began to print color woodcuts in a manner that recalls the scenic wallpapers of France and Alsace, where, starting about 1800, thousands of man-high wood blocks were combined in the most taxing technique ever used for block printing. After 1830 these wide expensive panoramas were priced out of the market by repeat

7. Pennsylvania state banknote, engraved by Jacob Perkins's process, Philadelphia, 1839.
*Martin Leifer Collection.*

designs quickly and cheaply turned out by new steam presses, rolling on endless ribbons of the new machine-made paper. This technological change must have thrown many block cutters and printers out of work, some of whom would seem to have immigrated to Boston, where their technique, a bit simplified, appears in the 1830s and 1840s on wallpapers, now mostly destroyed, on decorative panels for masking fireplaces in summer, and on coverings for hatboxes, which have often survived in attics. These boxes were pasted together in various places on the North Atlantic seaboard, using papers that sometimes bear the labels of the Boston printers John C. and Charles Cook, 1831 to 1836, and William Varnum, 1841 to 1847. Most of the hatbox papers showed decorative animals and flowers, but now and then adapted engravings and lithographs of well-known buildings (ill. 56) or the mechanical wonders of the age—the railroads, the innovative sailing ships, and the steamers.

### Westward Ho!

Americans put such a giant effort into ships, canals, and railroads because the very first settlers had immediately started to explore inland with a westward push that relentlessly gathered numbers and momentum until it at last burst all bounds in the Gold Rush of 1849. This westward migration, the greatest since the age of the Huns, resembled no other migration in being a mass movement of solitary individuals or families driving into a wilderness without government support, without a protecting army, with nothing to rely on for survival but a rifle, an axe, and courage. It is no wonder that the frontiersman made an instant legend of friendships and fighting, of dangers overcome, of forests massacred into fields, with every action huger than life (ill. 132). Yet even at the time, some people burlesqued the legend in rough woodcuts that still tickle our humor more than the partisan satire of political campaigns (ills. 21 – 23, 125).

### What the Frontiersman Left Behind

Making hatboxes was only one of the innumerable cottage industries that once busied whole families the world over during seasons that kept farmers and fishermen indoors. Today few families work together on commercial enterprises, but in 1791 Alexander Hamilton called the United States "a vast scene of household manufacturing."

However, the modern American factory system was already beginning. In 1785 Oliver Evans in Philadelphia constructed a water-driven flour mill so fully automated with conveyor belts that it needed no workman inside the mill to grind three hundred bushels of grain an hour. In 1798 Eli Whitney in New

Haven contracted to make ten thousand rifles, using drills and lathes so accurate that the parts of any gun would fit any other gun. Thus damaged guns could for the first time be easily repaired in the field. Four years before this, Whitney's invention of the cotton gin cleaned the seeds from fifty pounds (about twenty-five kilograms) of cotton in a day, instead of the one pound that could be cleaned by hand. This saving of labor made cotton such a profitable crop that it condemned the South to a one-crop agriculture, with all the attendant risks of unpredictable ruin, and made slaves a burden instead of a help. In 1822 cotton mills sprang up in open fields at Lowell, Massachusetts, near the Merrimack River. Eleven years later fifteen thousand Lowell workers were operating the world's most efficient textile mill, which took in raw cotton and wool at one end and turned out finished cloth at the other. By 1848 the United States was growing seven-eighths of the world's cotton, and cotton was every man's cloth instead of being an exotic fabric for the rich.

In 1843 the system of accurate, interchangeable parts was used to make clocks so cheap that 40,000 were exported all over the world. In clock factories each workman performed one operation in a production line that was to lead eventually to the Ford Motor Car factory at Willow Run. Since labor was scarce, workers had to be lured to the factories by tempting them with neat houses, a pleasant village-like community, with free lectures and concerts. Early American factories, driven by rapid streams, were very different from the British city factories, powered by coal—William Blake's "dark Satanic mills."

## The Bank of the United States in Early Cartooning

The United States factories' outpouring of flour, cloth, clocks, tools, chairs, carriages, reapers, locomotives, and God knows what else soon filled the seaside cities with handlers and insurers of goods in transit, who ran brisk countinghouses very like those in London or Amsterdam (ill. 58). Business prospered after Alexander Hamilton's brilliant reorganization of the government finances had brought a degree of prosperity that could not have been dreamed of during the wartime inflation. In 1791 he established the Bank of the United States with a twenty-year charter to help regulate the new nation's economy the way the Bank of England did for Britain. Even though it was not particularly effective, the American bank still proved so useful that after its charter lapsed in 1811, it was reestablished in 1816 for another twenty years.

Yet the Bank of the United States was disliked for a number of reasons: as a Federal bank, its notes circulated everywhere at par, thus restraining the hundreds of flighty little state banks, whose notes (ill. 7, 57) were worth less than par outside their state; the Bank of the United States seemed to farmers to be a group of rich city men selfishly using the bank to impose federal power at the expense of state autonomy; and finally, New York was jealous of so much finance being centered in Philadelphia. These regional discontents were excited and manipulated by Andrew Jackson, the first President who consistently ingratiated himself with the press, when he was campaigning in 1832 for a second term in the White House. At this inauspicious moment, the bank's arrogant director decided to force finance into a national issue by applying for a renewal of his charter then and there, four years before he had to. Congress approved the renewal, but Jackson was too publicly committed against the bank to be able to do anything except veto the charter bill (ill. 59). This left the whole country to seesaw from boom to panic with no balance wheel whatsoever until the National Bank Act was passed in 1863 to help pay for the Civil War. There was still no even partway effective stabilizer until the Federal Reserve Act was strengthened in 1935. Uncontrolled enterprise grew so prodigiously that the history of the United States in the nineteenth century is in large part the history of business. This explosive drive could not have made such headway without the Perkins method of engraving bank notes and stock certificates that were hard to forge.

## The Growth of Manufacturing

Business registered its growth in pictures of the various ways in which merchandise was offered for sale. The primitive European method of peddlers carrying their wares on foot was rare in the United States where farms lay too far apart for walking. Americans drove horse carts piled high with furniture, pots and pans, baskets, chairs, brooms, anything portable (ill. 8). A few of these itinerant peddlers built up some of the most important enterprises in the whole United States through stores that began modestly, and then grew in size and elaboration until they, like the great hotels, offered ordinary people the grandeur and opulence that churches and palaces provided in Europe. But in due time, even

13

the largest stores could not supply the multiple needs of so far-flung a country. So in 1872 Montgomery Ward in the country's railway center at Chicago started a mail-order business for direct distribution to lonely farms in order "to meet the wants of the patrons of Husbandry." Eighteen seventy-two was a propitious moment, for seven years of peace after the Civil War had settled the country. The war's need for gunboats, cannon, and railway rolling stock had created a heavy industry tooled to very exacting standards and powered by coal instead of falling water. The war-material factories promptly converted to making farm machinery, carriages, and sewing machines. The sewing machines in the North had just finished stitching the first factory-made army uniforms and now turned to revolutionizing civilian clothing. In an hour a machine in a factory could make a skirt that would take thirteen and half hours to sew by hand. Posters (ill. 76) were soon advertising inexpensive clothes of an elaboration such as had formerly bankrupted aristocrats in royal courts of rich countries. Ready-made clothes traveled thousands of miles over the new network of railways that also distributed fertilizers, reapers, and other newly invented farm machinery to the great plains of the Middle West. The resulting unprecedented crops of grain overflowed the United States in exports massive enough to flood the agriculture of Europe. The United States started to feed the world the way the Crimea had fed ancient Greece and Egypt fed Rome. Such a revolution in living conditions could hardly have happened unless the mail-order firms had found the necessary requirements in a huge country without custom barriers from the tropics to the Arctic, with adequate rail and ship connections, and a not entirely impossible postal system.

*Machines for the Home*

For the North American diversity of occupations and habitat, the mail-order houses had to offer a bewildering variety of articles inexpensively manufactured by quick and accurate automated machinery. In Europe, every advance in automation since the earliest power looms had met fierce resistance from employees afraid of being thrown out of work. But in the United States there were more jobs needing men than men needing jobs, so that factory workers were proud of the new machines and fascinated to learn how to operate them. In 1812/1813 Paul Svinin, the Russian traveler, had noticed the special laborsaving machines for cutting stone, cob-

bling shoes, molding bricks, and making nails.

A shortage of manpower— or womanpower—also organized American family life. This lack has now become endemic throughout almost all the Western world, but it appeared first in North America, where the dearth of domestic help has forced women in the United States to act as wife, mother, hostess, nurse, cook, housemaid, coachman or chauffeur in frantic succession. For this reason American women preceded European women in welcoming any device that could speed household drudgery to free them for more rewarding occupations. The great mail-order houses met this demand by offering American women a succession of newly invented, ever-more-perfected household appliances. The mail-order houses whetted the appetite of women by alluring advertisements of a smoother iron, a more versatile sewing machine, a more efficient clothes washer as though they were friends that no family could afford to be without (ills. 10, 11, 72 - 77, 83 - 85). When the new sewing machine is delivered, the whole family crowds to the door as if to welcome a long-lost uncle returning from the California goldfields (ills. 10, 11). Since a family can work efficiently together only when every member is feeling fit, many advertisements claimed methods of preventing disease instead of the European advertisements for cures for diseases already contracted (ill. 68). This attitude was already a sort of secular religion that continues today in the North American reliance on vitamins and exercise. In keeping with this feeling, American advertisers sometimes secularized traditional moral imagery (ills. 69, 70), though they more often dramatized the happy moments of a family working together (ills. 72 - 74). The humorous and human imagination of early advertising has since been lost in modern professionalism.

Nineteenth-century advertisers varied their presentations all the way from posters big enough to catch the eye of people across a wide street to thousands of little bright cards that tradesmen gave to customers for pasting into albums (ills. 78, 80, 81, 84, 85). Many sets of still smaller cards (ill. 79) were inserted into packs of cigarettes to persuade the smoker to continue buying the same brand of cigarettes in the hope of completing sets of a wide variety of subjects—Flags of All Nations, Heads of State, Scenes from Shakespeare, The Language of Flowers, Greek and Roman Gods and Goddesses, Nations of the World, Steamships, Wives of the Presidents, Inventions and Inventors, Governors of American States, Criminals Wanted Dead or Alive, Gymnastic Exercises, Occupations of Women, Actors and Actresses,

8. Wood engraving in *New York Cries in Rhyme*, New York, 1834. *Museum of the City of New York.*

**6**

**BASKETS! WOODEN BOWLS!**

*Jingle, jingle, jingle, goes a parcel of bells.*

Baskets, Wooden Bowls,
Of well chosen wood,
For a kitchen utensil
You'll find very good.

This is a useful business; for it supplies our kitchens with necessary articles, and takes in return our old iron, copper, lead, pewter, &c. The basket man has a waggon with uprights and cross-pieces, strung full with baskets and wares of different descriptions, making a great show, and calling the attention of the citizens by his numerous jingling bells.

These wares are made in great quantities in Connecticut, and along the New-York Grand Canal, and supply several Wooden Ware Stores in our city, with articles of little cost, but of much use.

Comic Characters like Mutt and Jeff, and a great many sets of Baseball Players. There could be no clearer inventory of the average American's mixture of interests.

### Color Lithography

Although chromolithographs for home decoration became common a decade or so after the end of the Civil War, commercial advertising was the big patron for color lithography. Advertisers used it for the big posters expertly printed in New York, Philadelphia, Boston, Chicago, and Cincinnati (ills. 72 - 77). Most posters were unsigned since no single designer dominated in the United States as Jules Chéret did in Paris. Black-and-white lithography was invented in Bavaria in the 1790s. Later, patents were issued in both Germany and France, and it was introduced into the United States where the first known lith-

ograph was published in 1819. The evocative color posters and trade cards gradually disappeared as advertisers turned to newspapers, radio, and finally television for their commercials, but the mail-order houses continued as of old to send out elaborate huge catalogues of hundreds of pages and thousands of illustrations—"wishing books," as they were called—that are encyclopedias of social history. Some of these bulky mail-order catalogues had holes punched in the upper left-hand corner for suspending them in outhouses where the thin pages got a final meditative look before being used as toilet paper.

### Advertising the Lure of the Road

Some manufacturers bypassed the mail-order houses and stores by selling directly from the factory to the customer through small illustrated catalogues. This was particularly the case with the makers of

9. Lithograph poster by Endicott, New York, 1850s.
*New-York Historical Society, Bella C. Landauer Collection.*

light carriages designed for rough country roads (ill. 16). These buggies and buckboards were not sprung on steel springs that broke easily and were hard to repair, but were suspended on thin boards of the flexible American ash and hickory. The carriage builders, like the shipbuilders, took advantage of the immense variety of American wood. Machines cut snug-fitting joints that did not shake apart when these practical carriages were exported to rough terrain in South America, India, and Australia (ill. 94). Skill in coachmaking had been growing ever since the eighteenth century, when only grand coaches (ill. 92) were imported, while farm carts were made at home.

The most famous farm wagon was the heavy, broad-wheeled vehicle, roofed with canvas, that was developed in Conestoga, Pennsylvania, before the Revolution, for carrying freight before the advent of railroads. Later it carried families over the Appalachians and eventually opened the West.

But the most sentimental conveyance was certainly the bicycle after the early, dangerous high wheeler (ill. 95) had been made light and safe in the 1890s to accommodate pairs of young people, rich and poor, in country and in city, who were bent on escaping and exploring. The bicycle struck the imagination of songwriters as no other mode of locomotion has ever done (ills. 97, 99). One of the many songs of the time was catchy enough for us still to hum unconsciously:

Daisy, Daisy, give me your answer true,
I'm half crazy, all for the love of you!
It won't be a stylish marriage,
I can't afford a carriage,
But you'll look sweet upon the seat
Of a bicycle built for two.

The skills that went into the making of bicycles, and carriages were then applied to making the early

10. Chromolithograph trade card, 1880s.
*New-York Historical Society, Bella C. Landauer Collection.*

automobiles (ill. 100). The automobile, however, never figured much in popular printmaking because it came when song sheets were beginning to be supplanted by recorded music, and it had to be advertised with sophistication to attract the few rich people who could then afford a conveyance that has now become everybody's accepted necessity.

*Ship Prints*

When American carriage building began in the eighteenth century, shipbuilding was also under way. Of all the manufactures that the early settlers brought with them from Europe, only two forged ahead of European standards—gunmaking and shipbuilding. Guns were essential for survival, used to shoot game for food and Indians when they attacked. Ships were needed in a then all but roadless country with interminable coasts and frequent harbors.

The geography of South America, on the contrary, discouraged travel by sea or by land. These countries had fewer rivers, many entangling jungles, isolating mountain ranges, and a Pacific coast of almost unbroken cliffs. But the United States invited ships to venture on the sea and then later on the convenient rivers. First, the sea. About 1750 Baltimore began to build schooners with sails set parallel to the keel so as to beat readily into the wind and to make the speed needed for smuggling sugar, rum, and slaves in the Caribbean trade. Even before the Revolution, these Baltimore schooners were bought by Britain, and during the War of 1812 they boldly and imperviously molested British ships in the very sight of British ports. Some time before this thoughtful, people had realized that a sea war with Britain or France was probably shaping up. But how could the infant Republic, which could afford to build no more than half a dozen ships, prepare itself to fight the hundreds of vessels in the great navies overseas? The unexpectedly successful solution was to design a ship midway between the two most formidable classes in the British navy, a ship that would look like a second-rate British ship, but would carry the heavy cannon of a first-rate ship on her upper decks only, counting on the probability that the enemy ship, with her heavy guns close to the water, would have to shut their low ports in rough weather, leaving available only the lighter guns on the upper deck. Thus the American ship could use

11. Chromolithograph trade card, 1880s.
*New-York Historical Society, Bella C. Landauer Collection.*

its heavy guns on its upper deck to hit the enemy while staying out of the range of the enemy's then available lighter guns. The American gamble succeeded, for in the War of 1812 each American ship was victorious unless she was trapped by a whole British fleet. The ship *Constitution* won so many victories that she may be said to have founded the United States Navy, which has preserved her to this day. The engraving of her is one of the liveliest of ship prints because it was designed by a ship's rigger, who knew each rope and stay by having planned them (ill. 104).

### Clipper Ship Cards

A new marine chapter had started in 1794 when the *Empress of China* sailed from New York for Canton to bring the United States into competition with the ancient European monopoly of trade with the Orient. The race was on for speed on the high seas, a race to take Canadian furs to Canton, Chinese tea to London, New England ice to Bombay, paddle-wheel ferries and portable houses from Boston and New York to San Francisco, and the whole world's manufactures to all North American ports. The race turned to a

stampede after the discovery of Californian gold late in 1848 lured adventurers westward from every country by any and every fast conveyance. The ships called clippers—a slang word for speedy—advertised their departures for San Francisco with pocket-sized cards lithographed in bright colors and tinted gold on coated paper like the trade cards that had been printed on similar *carton porcelaine* for several decades in Belgium (ills. 17, 18, 107, 108). Very likely these first elaborate American chromolithographs were printed by Belgian lithographers who had emigrated to Boston and New York during the European troubles of 1848. The sizes of a few American clipper cards are in even centimeters, not inches, showing that some of the cardboard, at least, must have been imported from Belgium.

### The Romance of the Sea

To sail around South America into the Pacific, the clipper ships had to go well in all the weathers encountered while crossing the temperate zones, the light airs of the horse latitudes, the hurricanes of the tropics, and the overwhelming Antarctic surges around the terrible Horn. To invent so versatile a

# Cabinet Ware Emporium.

The Subscribers would respectfully announce to the public that they have, at their large Ware-Rooms,

## NO. 136 SOUTH SECOND STREET, PHILADELPHIA,

One of the largest assortments in the United States of finished Furniture, of all descriptions known in the trade.

One of the partners devotes his whole time to the manufacturing department, preparing new patterns, and improving old ones, while the other gives his attention to the Upholstering and Finishing.

Such facilities in the Business give a decided superiority to all articles which they have to offer to the public.

### W. & J. ALLEN.

12. Wood-engraved advertisement, Philadelphia, 1855.
*New-York Historical Society.*

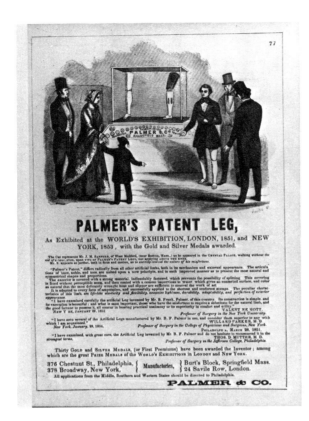

13. Wood-engraved advertisement, New York,
1855. *New-York Historical Society.*

14. Wood-engraved advertisement, New York, 1878.
*New-York Historical Society, Bella C. Landauer Collection.*

ship, New York and Boston builders began in the
1790s to experiment with hull design through so-
called lift models. These were carved in layers of
plank that were bolted together and then disassem-
bled to trace the form of the hull at various levels.
By towing models in water tanks, they discovered
that a long hull steadied the ship from pitching
when heading into surges, that sharp bows sweeping
upward in a hollow curve, called the cutwater,
sliced through waves instead of losing momentum
by battering at them in the speed gathered from sails
that towered skyward in tier on tier of canvas clouds.
In a few decades ship design changed as radically
as it had in all the previous 4,000 years. In the year
1853 when the clippers reached their peak, one hundred and ten were launched from Atlantic Coast
shipyards, and on a day of favoring wind some seventy might sail out of New York or Boston, while
over five hundred lay in San Francisco harbor where
their crews had jumped ship to adventure in the
goldfields, leaving the abandoned hulls to serve as
cheap hotels and warehouses. These last and most

glorious of commercial sailing ships commanded as
much attention as the public gives to queens and
movie stars today. Their records of speed astonished
like landings on the moon. The swiftness of these
extreme clippers has, indeed, never been surpassed
by commercial sail. Where ships before 1750 made
five or six knots, or at most ten, these clippers of a
century later raced up to twenty-two knots; sailed
465 sea miles in one day; 3,562 miles in eleven days.
Newspaper headlines proclaimed their record runs:
San Francisco to Canton in thirty-six days, Manila
to New York in eighty-four days, New York to
San Francisco in eighty-nine days, sixteen hours,
around the world in 194 days of actual sailing.
Their very names still make the heart skip a beat—
*Young America, Great Republic, Challenge, Red Jacket,
Golden Age, Westward Ho!, Southern Cross, Northern
Light, Glory of the Seas, Sea Witch, Flying Cloud,
Chariot of Fame, Herald of the Morning.* Though these
were some of the most imperial creations of all the
Americas, they ended after a bare decade of splendor,
leaving not a single survivor today. The clipper

20

15. Chromolithograph poster, Philadelphia, 1880s.
*New-York Historical Society, Bella C. Landauer Collection.*

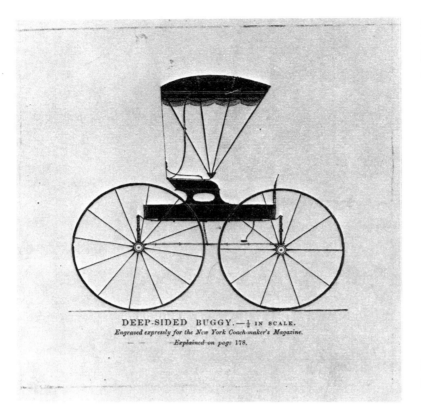

DEEP-SIDED BUGGY.—⅛ IN SCALE.
Engraved expressly for the New York Coach-maker's Magazine.
—Explained on page 178.

ships were killed by the first worldwide panic of 1857, the Civil War of 1861–1865, and finally in 1869 by the double blow of the Transcontinental Railway that supplanted the sea route to California, and the opening of the Suez Canal that shortened the way to the Orient through waters that po not favor sailing. The mastery of the seas passed to England's prosaic, grimy, plodding but punctual steamships. Actually, these last great sailing ships were obsolete before they slid down the ways into the water. Some awareness of this fact became a part of the romantic appeal that inspired many pictures of them (ills. 103, 106). Indeed, it must have needed all the infatuation of rapture to sustain the clipper crews through the hazard, in gale winds, of reefing sails thirty or forty yards (meters) above the decks and the waves, suffering the sores of scurvy and epidemics of typhus, while submitting to the lash of the discipline needed to break records of speed.

*Racing Yachts*

Out of all this maritime inventiveness in North America nothing now survives but one useless craft, the racing yacht. Modern racing design started in 1851 when Prince Albert had assembled the arts and crafts of the world in the Great Exhibition at the Crystal Palace in London, and then proposed to match this with the sports of the world. At his request, the Royal Yacht Squadron at Cowes invited foreign yacht clubs to race in August around the Isle of Wight. When this challenge reached the New York Yacht Club, its president, Commodore John Cox Stevens, resolved to meet it by building an enlarged version of the swift and sturdy pilot boats that met ships in the open ocean to steer them into New York harbor. When the *America* (ill. 105), as she was christened, dropped anchor at Cowes, the novelty of her lines and rigging made one British yachtsman remark that either he or she must be mad. In the event, however, the *America* crossed the finish line nearly half an hour ahead of the next boat and won the America's Cup for the New York Yacht Club to hold until a contender should sail the Atlantic and win on the New York course. The trophy is still in New York. In astonishment at the victory, Queen Victoria boarded the *America* with a party of yachtsmen who discreetly inspected the hull for hidden engines. The *America*, bought by a British yachtsman, became the prototype of the Liverpool pilot boats and the grandparent

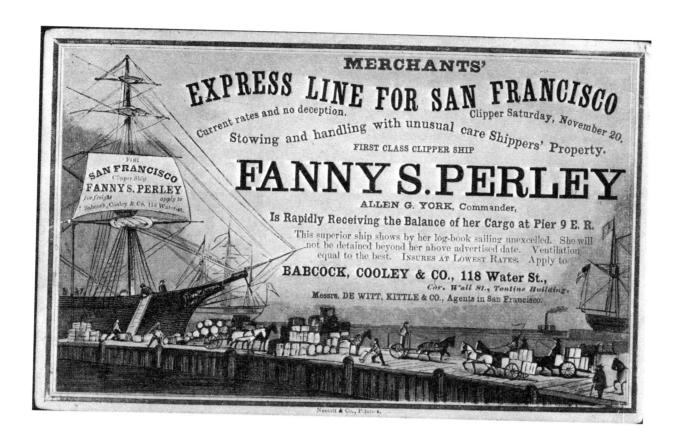

of modern racing craft. These latter have now developed to such a luxurious point of uselessness that a yacht fast enough to win on the New York course against local boats has no storage room or living quarters for a crew to sail her across the Atlantic. Acknowledging this, the New York Yacht Club no longer requires contenders to sail the Atlantic in their own bottoms. Modern specifications have made these racing machines too costly for any single individual, no matter how rich, to build and operate one, so that this competitive display may in time follow the clipper ship into oblivion.

### Riverboats on the Hudson

Sailing ships kept the United States in touch with countries overseas, but were hampered in many rivers by swirling shallows and by the difficulty of tacking and turning about. New Yorkers therefore took up European experiments with propulsion by steam. In 1804 John Stevens, the father of the John Cox Stevens who sponsored the *America*, discovered that paired screw propellors, revolving in opposite directions, drove a boat in a straight line and made it easier to steer. This discovery could not be put to practical use until steam engines developed pressure enough to turn propellors really fast. But propellors need fairly deep water to work efficiently, requiring a hull too deep for many American rivers. For navigation on river shallows, Stevens took up the idea of the paddle wheel that had been known, like the mill wheel, since the late Roman Empire. But whereas falling water has force enough to make the mill wheel immediately useful, the paddle wheel needed more than muscle power to propel a boat with any practical speed. John Stevens geared paddle wheels to a fairly strong steam engine in his *Phoenix*, intended for service on the Hudson. Before he could launch her, the monopoly for the Hudson River had been seized by Robert Fulton for his paddle-wheeler *Clermont* (ill. 111), so in 1809 Stevens steered his *Phoenix* to Philadelpia, in the first ocean voyage ever risked by a steamship, and Fulton started a steamship's first regular schedule of passenger service between New York and Albany. While screw propellors drive a boat really efficiently in one direction only, paddle wheels work equally well in either direction. For this reason paddle wheels survived on New York ferry boats that the Civil War pressed into service as gunboats to run up and down narrow southern rivers.

18. Advertisement for private flags of New York merchants, 1839.
*New-York Historical Society.*

*Riverboats on the Mississippi*

In 1816 a New Orleans builder invented the Mississippi riverboat by constructing several decks on top of a flat-bottomed, shallow-draft barge. It was said that such boats could skim for a mile on the foam from a keg of beer, which was what was required on the vast river and some forty tributaries whose current turned drowned trees and restlessly shifted mud shoals until pilots found that the river was never the same as before. Wood fuel for the journey of 2,000 or 3,000 miles (3,000 or 4,000 kilometers) could be picked up along the forested riverbanks. The Mississippi boats became the vastest of all paddle-wheelers, carrying a thousand passengers inside the tiers of decks stacked solid with bales of cotton and hogsheads of tobacco—nearly twice the tonnage that clipper ships carried overseas. These inland riverboats that were never buffeted by waves

could afford to splurge with more flagrant ornamentation than even Nero's barges or the *Bucentaur*. Their grand saloons (ill. 109), nearly a hundred yards (meters) long, were dream palaces of Gothic arcades, grand staircases, carved mahogany, gold-framed pictures, flowered carpets, marble-topped tables, deep upholstery, crystal chandeliers, cut glass, and plated silver, all enjoyed to the strains of digestive adagios from a parlor organ. The weeks spent on the Mississippi riverboats were rarely dull, for there were always glossy professional gamblers and cardsharps to attract passengers with bright talk while they fleeced them of their money, and these boats often raced each other for the prize of the river, a pair of stag antlers—the buckhorns—that the fastest boat suspended between the twin smokestacks (ill. 112). In 1853 a riverboat steamed upstream against the strong current for 1,024 miles in three days, averaging fourteen knots (22 kilometers an hour). Speed brought danger when boilers exploded and snags of sunken trees ripped the flat wooden bottoms. In the first thirty-three years of riverboat history, 235 Mississippi boats sank or blew up, killing some twenty-five hundred people. All these grand floating palaces have vanished, leaving nothing but a modest boat or two that still plie the great river for nostalgic pleasure cruises. Our illustration shows an equally modest cabin of one of the humbler Hudson riverboats (ill. 65).

## Canals

Success with shipping influenced Americans to supplement river transportation by digging canals rather than by building railways, like the British. After opening several successful small canals, the great Erie Canal was dug for 350 miles in eight years to carry cheap water freight between the port of New York and the Great Lakes. During the year after the opening in 1825, the locks were working day and night to pass nineteen thousand boats. A decade of this active traffic created the city of Buffalo at the Lake Erie end of the canal, and at the other end founded the commercial supremacy of New York City where ocean freight had to break bulk. The leisurely reverie of canal travel inspired a whole folklore of songs as well as many pictures. Charles Dickens vividly described his days and nights on the Erie Canal in 1841:

> Even the running up, bare-necked, at five o'clock in the morning, from the tainted cabin to the dirty deck, scooping up the icy water, plunging one's head into it, and drawing it out, all fresh and glowing with color, was a good thing. The fast, brisk walk upon the towing-path, between that hour and breakfast, when every vein and artery seemed to tingle with health; the exquisite beauty of the opening day, when light came gleaming out from everything; the lazy motion of the boat, when one lay idly on the deck, looking through, rather than at, the deep blue sky; the gliding on at night, so noiselessly, past frowning hills, sullen with dark trees, and sometimes angry in one red, burning spot high up, where unseen men lay crouching around a fire; the shining out of the bright stars undisturbed by noise of wheels or steam, or any other sound than the limpid rippling of the water as the boat went on were pure delights.

## Railway Prints

In 1811 during the first success of canals, John Stevens, as a lonely prophet, had vainly urged the building of railways instead. When railways were finally started, the tracks often paralleled the level route of the canals. North American railways lacked the benefit of the governmental, mostly military, planning that coordinated the railway systems of Europe. Any American who thought that he could make money went right ahead and laid tracks from any factory to the nearest freight wharf, or from any town to any other town in a chaos of short lines with eight different gauges. The carriages were simply the bodies of horse coaches mounted on different wheels (ill. 115). Horses pulled the light train almost as fast as the locomotive when it rained hard enough to dampen the locomotive's firebox. The total track of the first ninety-five railways added up to a mere forty-one miles, but there were 2,800 miles of track by 1840, 30,000 miles by 1860, despite a pause during the panic of 1857, and in the all-time peak decade of the 1880s about 70,000 miles of new track were added.

By 1860 the railways were consuming about one-half of the American production of iron and steel, and they dominated the business world. American factories exported locomotives to Germany and Austria, and in 1854 made a steam shovel for the British railways. Between 1844 and 1850 the father of James Abbott McNeill Whistler, the painter, engineered the 420-mile line between St. Petersburg and Moscow, and equipped it with rolling stock made in Russia under American supervision. Unification of the disconnected lines proceeded in earnest when the Civil War in 1861 turned into the first conflict to oppose one region's entire industry against another's, and the first to transport more war materiel by railway than by horses. The spread of railways depended greatly on the inexpensive, easily assembled bridges constructed with the truss patented by Ithiel Town that enabled wide spans to be bridged with short timbers (ill. 118). Railways changed American eating habits by bringing seafood inland (ill. 119), by distributing meat from the Chicago slaughter-houses after refrigerator cars were invented in 1868, and by conveying oranges from Florida and California.

Yet American railway travel did not invite the weak. Charles Dickens in 1841 described conditions that would daunt the strongest of us today:

> There is a gentlemen's car and a ladies' car;

the main distinction between which is that in the first everybody smokes; and in the second, nobody does. As a black man never travels with a white one, there is also a negro car, which is a great, blundering, clumsy chest.... In the center of the carriage there is usually a stove, fed with charcoal or anthracite coal; which is for the most part red hot. It is insufferably close; and you see the hot air fluttering like the ghost of smoke.

During the first years of the Transcontinental Railway trains had to halt for hours to let thousands of buffalo dawdle across the tracks, though "sportsmen" soon came near to exterminating the herds by shooting at random from the speeding trains. In blizzards the men passengers got out to shovel snow (ill. 120), and at the infrequent twenty-minute stops only the ruthless succeeded in bolting a few indigestible bites (ill. 124). But the competition of the various lines stimulated inventors to design a few minimal comforts. In 1858 the first sleeping car left Chicago with cots that were lowered by ropes from the ceiling. The inventor, George Pullman, soon refined the idea by springing the upper beds entirely out of sight by day and by sliding adjustable seats to become lower beds by night. The sleeping car suddenly became fashionable when Mrs. Lincoln ordered one for her own use on the train that carried the body of her murdered husband through the chief northern cities.

In 1867 Pullman built the first dining car, with a galley contrived as compactly as a Swiss watch. When dining cars began to serve meals as elaborate as the best hotels, they became the smartest places to eat, in surroundings of marquetry walls, brocaded upholstery, and electrically lighted glass that rivaled the old riverboats in gorgeousness if not in size. The American love affair with the clipper ships transferred itself to the trains, giving them personal names like Yankee Clipper, Super Chief, Merchants' Limited, Denver Zephyr, Forty-Niner, City of San Francisco, Night Owl, East Wind, Silver Meteor.

A train seemed just the thing to convey the allure of high fashion in clothing (ill. 117). Trains encouraged travel by organizing the first collegiate rowing race in New England in 1852, by stopping to let passengers pick blueberries in the pastures, and by running onto piers beside beaches and pleasure boats (ill. 20). But when Americans turned to their next love, the automobile, the trains were gradually abandoned to their present ignominy of dirt and dilapidation. Now that the automobile in turn is losing its glamour, the next comer—the airplane—is not taking it up. Both have dwindled to mere conveniences for getting somewhere.

*Lithography in California*

To help investors finance railways, the government granted them land along the tracks for the venturer to sell off for homesteads and towns. But everywhere beyond the new settlements stretched the wilderness, where the trapper and the frontiersman survived by being the Indians' best pupils. Their deeds became an instant legend, the subject of woodcuts that still tickle our fancy with their rough-and-ready humor (ills. 21-23, 125). These were the footloose adventurers who led the way to California when gold was found late in 1848, to be followed by a rush of the discontented from all over the world. Few of the forty-niners made money in the goldfields, but many did well for themselves by providing goods and services as San Francisco grew from a population of 3,000 in 1846 to a reputed 125,000 in 1850.

Suddenly new forms of government had to be improvised there and in the plank-and-canvas cities that sprang up in a few months and were as recklessly abandoned when the gold vein gave out. Many of the forty-niners were young dropouts from eastern schools who had hardly enough education to write a letter home. But even if you were the glibbest of writers, how could you tell your mother that nothing much was happening? That you had not made even the first penny of your fortune? That you would give all the tea in China to be at home with her again? Help for the embarrassment of these nonwriters was offered by several San Francisco lithographers who imported thin, often blue, letter paper from Europe, folded it once, and filled the first page with a picture of California life (ills. 127-129, 132). Since there were no envelopes, the address took up the back page, leaving only the two inner pages for a brief message that could comment impersonally on what was shown in the picture. Though these pictorial letter sheets are rare now, they sold in quantities for five cents each and gave the whole world its first look at the goldfields, with their life of drudgery, of hope and disappointment, of rowdy, sad gambling in the shanty towns, the edginess of men without women, the erupting murders, and the mob violence of hangings by the Vigilante Committee (ill. 130).

Yet in a surprisingly few years San Francisco set-

19. Little Rollo on the steam boat. Wood engraving in Jacob Abbott: *Rollo's Travels*, Philadelphia, 1841. *New York, Metropolitan Museum of Art, gift of William M. Ivins, Jr.*

tled into more or less usual city ways. The smart stores began to advertise with smooth lithographs ordered from New York (ill. 133) and the shacks gave way to fancy clubs and newfangled skating rinks (ills. 24, 25). But the upstart elegance said good-bye to the boisterous vitality that animates the first lithographs. In these first efforts the rough drawing and sloppy printing had to make their effect in plain black and white because San Francisco, unlike New York, then had no women able to tint prints with watercolors.

California lithography was founded by the partnership of Britton & Rey. Joseph Britton was born in 1825 in Yorkshire and when he was ten, came to New York, where he was signing lithographs in 1847. He joined the Gold Rush when he was twenty-four in the first party to take a shortcut across the Isthmus of Panama through Lake Nicaragua to a ship up the Pacific Coast. In 1852, after frustrated attempts at mining, he set up a lithographic publishing house with Jacques Joseph Rey, an Alsatian

five years older than Britton, who had studied painting, lithography, and the piano in Europe, had visited Russia as courier and secretary to a wealthy traveler, and had then come to California by way of Panama, though not, apparently, to prospect for gold. In 1852 he and Britton began to issue lithographs together, and in 1855 Rey married Britton's sister. The household that the three kept together became a center for the musical and artistic life of San Francisco. The partnership of Britton & Rey lasted until Rey's death. Britton carried on alone until Rey's son Valentine was old enough to take his father's place. We would know more about Britton & Rey if the firm's records had not been destroyed in the terrible earthquake of 1906. Though Britton signed some of the prints alone (ill. 127), he is said to have been the business head, leaving Rey to do most of the drawing. The two made livelier lithographs than most of the Atlantic Coast firms because they designed the subjects and drew them themselves on the stone.

When Britton & Rey started their lithographic press in San Francisco, the process had been current for half a century, during which it developed a different character in each country. In Germany, where lithography had been invented in the 1790s, romantic artists had used it to dramatize Gothic buildings and to copy Gothic paintings and drawings. France alone had the artistic wit to perceive that the new process did not just substitute inexpensively for the old line engraving in copying paintings, but that it for the first time enabled a painter to multiply his most personal inventions by drawing on stone as freely and freshly as he drew on paper. The English perfected chromolithography by exactly superimposing many colors from as many stones, and they used their expertness for children's books as well as for commercial work. The United States mostly followed Britain. Though a New Yorker was experimenting with imported stones and ink by 1808, the first now known American lithograph was published in Philadelphia in 1819, the remarkable year when the return of peace after Napoleon's wars allowed lithography to burst forth productively in France and Germany. Soon North American lithography began to record the most dramatic moments of the century-long explosion that transformed the continent convulsively, drastically, irresistibly, and at breakneck speed.

## Currier & Ives

While hundreds of small lithographic presses came and went in the eastern states, the one preponderant firm of Currier & Ives flourished for sixty years at various addresses on Nassau Street in New York. Much has been written about Currier & Ives, for they were by all odds the most energetic and successful print publishers who have ever worked in the Americas. Through mail-order catalogues and traveling agents they pushed their lithographs out of New York to the Pacific, into South America, across Europe, and down to Australia. They invaded foreign markets by adapting to foreign tastes, by printing religious subjects like Madonnas and the Sacred Heart with titles in Spanish. Their nearly seven thousand prints constitute one of the longest inventories known for print publishers anywhere. Just bulk alone makes their achievement impossible to dislodge from history.

This success story started by accident. In 1828 a fifteen-year-old boy, Nathaniel Currier, went from his native Roxbury, Massachusetts, to nearby Boston. There he got a job as printer's devil under the Pendleton brothers, who had started America's first really successful lithographic firm about three years before. As luck would have it, the Pendletons' French pressman was the first competent and professional lithographic printer to come to the United States, and so could ground young Nathaniel in that tradition of clean printing for which the French have long been famous. When Nathaniel was twenty-two his shrewd good-humored energy drove him to New York, where he started out with a partner but soon set up for himself. He turned out the job printer's usual run of billheads, trade cards, views of cities, and sentimental pinup girls until he was twenty-seven, when a spectacular news event gave him his chance.

On the evening of January 13, 1840, the steamer *Lexington* was running from New York to Stonington, Connecticut, where passengers bound for Boston changed to the short railway line. About midnight the *Lexington*'s boilers were fired so hot that the smokestack ignited the wood around it. The captain tried to head the blazing paddle-wheeler landward, but the tiller ropes had charred through and the engines stopped when she was two miles offshore. There 123 persons burned to death or were drowned in the icy chop of Long Island Sound. Four men saved their lives by straddling bales of cotton, adrift from the ship's cargo, and hanging on until the tardy January dawn. Three days after the news reached New York, Currier published a lithographed broadside *The Extra Sun*, gaudy with a picture of midnight flames, that was hawked all over town by newsboys and peddlers (ill. 113). Currier's scoop in pictorial journalism made such a nationwide impression that he was getting orders for the *Lexington* lithograph eleven months after the disaster. For sixty years after this first success in merchandising, pushcart peddlers called each morning at Nassau Street for prints, paid a deposit, and returned the unsold prints in the evening.

This apt disaster capped Currier's dozen years of experience and enabled him to launch his business on a new national, and ultimately international, footing. He continued to issue news pictures when they were warranted by conspicuous events like the trotting race between the horses Peytona and Fashion in 1845, or the burning of Richmond that ended the Civil War (ill. 163). But he early established the variety of subjects that the firm advertised in 1870 as "Juvenile, Domestic, Love Scenes, Kittens

20. Chromolithograph travel poster, New York, 1880s.
*New-York Historical Society.*

and Puppies, Ladies Heads, Catholic Religious, Patriotic, Landscapes, Vessels, Comic, School Rewards and Drawing Studies, Flowers and Fruits, Motto Cards, Horses, Family Registers, Memory Pieces and Miscellaneous in great variety, and all elegant and salable Pictures."

In 1852 Currier coped with the rapid growth of his business by hiring a bookkeeper, eleven years younger than he, whose name was James Merritt Ives. Young Ives proceeded to examine much more than his ledgers as he quickly developed a shrewd eye for the public taste in pictures. In 1857 they formed a partnership that lasted until 1880 when Currier retired. After Ives in his turn retired in 1895, the firm declined until the terminal auction in 1907.

As long as Currier worked in the firm, he had the lithographs printed by the same simple process that he had learned in his youth. Professional lithographic draftsmen translated a designer's sketch or painting into lines and tones that made the stone easy to print. The black-and-white prints were then colored by hand. For rush orders, the colors were painted on by girls lined up at long tables in the shop, each one brushing on one color as the prints passed through her hand. If time did not matter, prints were colored by women painting at home for the miserable pay of one cent for small prints, and one dollar a dozen for big ones. Four hundred years before, the Gothic woodcuts must have been colored by methods quite as simple. In the old woodcuts, as in the lithographs, the black serves merely to guide the paint brush and the white requires coloring to keep the print from looking thin. After Currier retired in 1880, Ives began to keep up with developments in lithography by printing each color from a separate stone to speed production and to achieve the brilliant blending of waterproof colors required for the firm's new line of "Illuminated Pictorial Posters" (ill. 170). Since the firm was not equipped to print in colors, these chromolithographs had to be printed outside. Though "chromo" has become a term of contempt, the process was used for some of Currier & Ives's most striking prints.

The firm bought rough sketches for one dollar to ten dollars each, and paid considerably more for oil paintings. The staff lithographers who then copied these designs onto the stone, often divided up the work—one copying the trees, another the figures, a third the architecture, and so on. The designer rarely touched the stone to vary the dead level of neatness. This division of labor survived from the old industrial engravers who copied paintings because their burin technique was too specialized for

painters to learn. Nathaniel Currier clearly proclaimed the origins of his practice when he advertised his lithographs as ENGRAVINGS FOR THE PEOPLE. The typical designer for Currier & Ives, or at least the ideal one from their point of view, was a little English lady called Frances Flora Bond Palmer. Fanny Palmer was born in Leicester in 1812, where she received the usual genteel girl's education in the piano, singing, drawing, and modeling wax flowers. In her thirties she came to New York, where she found she had to support her alcoholic husband and a sister. Somehow she got to Currier & Ives, who commissioned her to draw every conceivable kind of subject until she died in 1876. They drove her to Long Island marshes so that she could sketch backgrounds for scenes of bird shooting, but she was equally willing to turn her hand to all kinds of things that she can never have seen with her own eyes, such as western trains, Indians, and boat races on the Missisippi (ill. 112). But this cozy little English lady's specialty lay in scenes of rural contentment, with neat, square white houses, elm trees, and smoothly raked curving carriage drives (ill. 134).

Currier & Ives standardized their prints in two sizes to facilitate packing in bulk shipments, and to fit two kinds of standard frames for display in salesrooms and for selling to customers. They put their most careful drawing into the big prints (22 by 28 inches) that retailed for a dollar and a half to three dollars. Less of the original designer's vision survives in the small prints 16 by 20 inches that sold to poorer people for fifteen to twenty cents each. It is the big prints that almost always flash to the eye of memory at the mention of Currier & Ives. Did the richer buyers look more at *how* a picture was drawn and the poorer ones at *what* was drawn? Or did the firm think that their more striking designs deserved publishing in a larger format? Whatever the reason, the fact remains that Currier & Ives lithographs are one of the few categories of art in which size has something to do with excellence.

In all this vast and varied production, Europeans seem to have fastened most on a series of about a hundred lampoons of black people in outrageous costumes called the Darktown Comics. Nowadays they look painfully racist, but they must have had appeal abroad as exotics. France alone bought 73,000 impressions. But except when laughing in a superior way, Currier & Ives turned their backs on the banal brutality of much of American life in order to concentrate on what Americans wished they were. The snug cottages and friendly leisure of their country scenes idealize the United States as much as the posters

21. Wood engraving in *Davy Crockett's Almanac*, New York, 1844.
*New York, Metropolitan Museum of Art.*

22. Wood engraving in *Davy Crockett's Almanac*, New York, 1844.
*New York, Metropolitan Museum of Art.*

RIDING A WHALE.

23. Wood engraving in *Davy Crockett's Almanac*, New York, 1850.
*New York, Metropolitan Museum of Art.*

for sewing machines (ill. 77). Thus it is hard for an American to judge Currier & Ives lithographs because we stand too close to see them clearly, and we read the stories of our grandparents in them. But no one could help being charmed by the freshness of an innocent eye, and often by the rush with which they dramatized a great age as it was gathering speed.

### Lithography in Philadelphia

Contented, busy, prosperous city life became a typical theme for lithography in Philadelphia, possibly because the city had, and still has, such a strong tradition of wealth and benefactions. By 1750 William Penn's colony of sober, industrious, and mutually helpful Quakers had become the second English-speaking city after London in point of elegance and culture. Non-Philadelphians have said that Philadelphia is not so much a city as a state of mind, a preoccupation with its own affairs, some of which one may glimpse in the lithographs scattered through these pages (ills. 32, 38, 110, 115, 118, 138). These

evocations of a very individual local life were drawn by many lithographers, among whom one stands out for giving his figures more importance than their setting (ills. 55, 138). This was Augustus Köllner who was born in 1813 in Düsseldorf and trained there in the academy that produced many painters for the United States and Russia. When he was twenty-six or twenty-seven, he came to the United States, where he must have traveled widely to draw views of fifty-one cities that were published by Goupil in Paris in 1848. By then he had already settled in Philadelphia, where he continued to draw lithographs until the 1870s. His liveliest prints were published about 1850 by the American Sunday School Union in booklets called *Common Sights in Town* and *Common Sights for Country Eyes*. These are among the few American pictures that try to record life as it is instead of striving to show what it should, or should not, be. Such a clear-eyed examination of one's surroundings is the exception in the English-speaking world, though it has provided the French with repeated inspiration in painting and in writing. Köllner looked around him at the leisurely life in the wide, uncluttered Philadelphia streets and drew

24. Lithograph cigar box label, San Francisco, 1870.
*New York, Metropolitan Museum of Art.*

the people, the horses, the commercial carts as lucidly as Adam Klein was then doing around Nuremberg. Köllner's lithographs are among the very few in the eastern United States that say "I was there" as distinctly as the California lithographs do, and Köllner said it more easily.

### *Fire! Fire!*

In the wooden North American cities that Köllner drew, the most exciting spectacle was a fire. Many travelers looked forward to a chance of seeing this early American display that was made famous when whole cities burned almost to the last house. Chicago disappeared twice in flames, which partly accounts for the city's reckless boldness in experimenting with architectural innovations.

In the early 1840s Sir Charles Lyell described a typical American fire in Philadelphia:

> We were five days here, and every night there was an alarm of fire, usually a false one; but the noise of the firemen was tremendous.

At the head of the procession came a runner blowing a horn with a deep unearthly sound, next a long team of men (for no horses are employed) drawing a strong rope to which the ponderous engine was attached with a large bell at the top, ringing all the way; next followed a mob, some with torches, others shouting loudly; and before they were half out of hearing, another engine follows with a like escort; the whole affair resembles a scene in *Der Freischütz* or *Robert le Diable*, rather than an act in real life.

When a fireman was a hero as conspicuous as an opera singer, he naturally became a favorite subject for pictures (ill. 141), and even his fire engine was worth painting as elaborately as an opera backdrop (ill. 139). A particularly impressive fire was the one that destroyed the New York Crystal Palace in 1858, only five years after it had been built on Fifth Avenue at Forty-second Street, then the north end of the town (ills. 136, 140). The fires that consumed the three great steel-and-glass Crystal Palaces constructed in London, New York, and Munich were

33

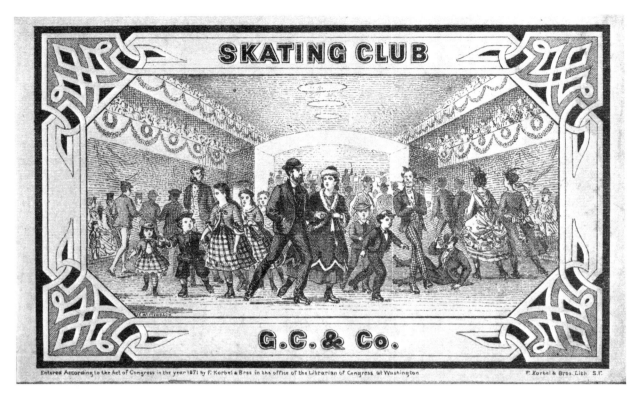

25. Lithograph cigar box label, San Francisco, 1871.
*New York, Metropolitan Museum of Art.*

all particularly violent because the vast halls enclosed enough air to feed the blaze until the heat melted the glass to admit more air.

### Shakers and Camp Meetings

Outside of the towns, travelers looked for a sight of the various religious sects. Of these the most famous was perhaps the Shakers, an offshoot from the Quakers in England, who had emigrated to form a community in upper New York State in 1787. From there they soon spread into New England and a little into the South. They were called Shakers because they writhed and trembled when they were "wrestling in soul to be freed from the power of sin and a worldly life." Our picture (ill. 142) shows some overdressed tourists watching them dance and dangle their hands to shake the evil out of their souls. They have cleared the floor for their dancing by hanging the furniture on pegs driven into the walls. Since they believed that God is bisexual, Shaker women shared equally with men in ruling their remote celibate communities, where all kept busy farming, making furniture, knitting clothes, weaving linen, marketing garden seed in labeled packets (then a novelty), and inventing ingenious cow barns and machines for peeling apples and making nails. Unlike many Protestant sects, the Shakers showed an interest in art by drawing pretty designs in devotional manuscripts and by working local woods into light, strong, practical furniture whose clean lines anticipate our taste today.

City-dwelling Protestant sects gathered during the summer in pretty woodlands, often near lakes, and lived in tents to attend camp meetings (ill. 143). A minister would rouse them by preaching and by leading them in singing until they triumphed over their troubles in a release of their whole being. A traveler was awed by the power of this mass ecstasy:

> The noise was like the roar of Niagara. The vast sea of human beings seemed to be agitated as if by a storm. Some of the people were singing, others praying, some crying for mercy in the most piteous accents, while others were shouting. At one time I saw at least five hundred people swept down in a moment, as if a battery of a thousand guns had opened upon them. Then immediately followed shrieks and shouts that rent the very heavens.

34

*Lithographed Song Sheets*

Americans made more music in the nineteenth century than they do now, for many were taught music in school, and all sang hymns every Sunday in church and popular songs during the week at home. Such was their longing for music that after a typical settler in the West had roofed and glazed his house, his next requirement was an upright piano or a parlor organ around which the family and the neighbors could gather for singing. The public demand for song sheets busied many small lithographic presses from about 1820 until after 1900 when recorded music and then the radio discouraged home performers.

Few song sheets were lithographed in Philadelphia, where the Quakers worshipped by meeting in silence until the spirit moved a member to speak, but in Boston, New York, Baltimore, and Cincinnati church singing created a public that devoured all kinds of sheet music. After Boston printed the first song sheet with a pictorial cover, these began to appear by the hundreds, priced at twenty-five to seventy-five cents each, as favorite gifts from a young man to his best girl. Music covers record the range of American worries, dreams, and aspirations, from hymn singing at home (ill. 26) to anxiety for the men of the family exposed to danger as sailors on the clipper ships (ills. 144, 146), the rowdiness of being all boys together in the saloon (ill. 145), the fear of being thrown down the front stoop by the girl of his dreams (ill. 27).

Many music covers show slender young men in tinsel uniforms strutting through drills as prim as minuets performed to the so-called "quick step" of one hundred and twenty steps to the minute (ill. 28, 29, 147, 148). This innocent-looking charade produced a mood of militarism that led to the arrogant seizure of northern Mexico in 1848. When Irishmen were being hanged for agitating home rule in the 1880s, some of their most violent supporters were Irish Americans (ill. 149).

The designers of the song-sheet covers remained obscure unless, like Winslow Homer in Boston, they went on to make a name by becoming painters.

*Naive Printmakers*

All the time that these well-trained lithographers were working in the cities, many self-taught "naive" painters and silhouette cutters were traveling in the country to record faces. The most skillful early North American silhouettist was William Henry Brown who excelled in catching the exact weight, balance, and gesture of men (never women) with about ten minutes of cutting, for which he charged one dollar—considerably more than the usual price for a silhouette. He boasted that he could cut recognizable likenesses of strangers seen in the street several hours before. His intelligent conversation kept his sitters looking lively and brought him in contact with many prominent people. He lithographed his profiles of twenty-seven of his most outstanding subjects in a book that was almost entirely destroyed in a warehouse fire (ill. 153). We illustrate his portrait of John Randolph, the last surviving signer of the Declaration of Independence, on his Virginia plantation. Although Brown cut large scenes like an entire fire company with its engine, and a railway train complete with locomotive and passengers in every coach, he probably could not make a living from his art, for when he was fifty-one he gave it up to work for a railroad.

There are practically no printmakers to match the charm of the itinerant painters who went about making pictures of faces, farms, and homesteads. Their patrons wanted paintings to hang in their parlors, but had no use for prints. Almost the only naive engraver was a certain George White who lived mostly in Bennington, Vermont, and worked a couple of copperplates with tools used by decorators of silverware. He engraved zigzag lines with a chase that rocked back and forth to brighten a silver surface with tracks of sparkle (ill. 150).

The only very personal naive printmaker derived at least part of his originality from ineptitude. This was the "Reverend" William Cook of Salem, Massachusetts, who studied theology, though he seems never to have been ordained as a minister. He made his living by giving private lessons in Latin, Greek, and mathematics. In 1852, when he was forty-five he got some discarded newspaper type and began to print about forty booklets of his really quite dreadful verses. He illustrated them with little blocks, of birch or maple that he hacked with his jackknife and printed so imperfectly that he had to finish most of the impressions with pencil (ills. 31, 151, 152). He cannot have done much more than recoup the cost of his materials by selling his booklets, bound in discarded scraps of cotton, to his pupils and to passers-by on the quiet Salem streets. His intention reminds one of course of William Blake, but with this enormous difference: where Blake was soundly trained in conventional techniques that he then discarded to achieve new effects, the Reverend Mr. Cook's undeniable charm comes from his struggle with uninstructed awkwardness. Yet when he adapts an engraving of a baroque masterpiece, like Guillaume Coustou's *Horses of Marly*, his rough cutting actually clarifies the grandeur of the original design (ill. 31).

*Propaganda against Alcohol and Slavery*

The "Reverend" Mr. Cook represented a moral point of view that found expression in many popular prints issued to combat the bad American habit of obsessive drinking (ill. 155). The agitation against hard liquor finally led to the unenforceable era of Prohibition in 1920–1933. The early campaigns against drink dramatized its damage to the earning power of the poor, whereas compulsive drinking appears today as the demoralizer of anybody's personality.

The other, and much more passionate, American crusade combatted slavery. In 1619 when the first slave ship landed in Virginia—the blackest day in American history—the slave trade had been going on in Latin America for nearly a century in an established pattern as African chiefs sold their captives to white middlemen. Through slavery the only Americans who were transported against their will were forced into a population that had adventured forth with a drive to construct a world more to their liking. This disparity of purpose separates blacks and whites more than any difference of color. Jefferson wanted to abolish slavery through the Constitution, but had to delete the clause when South Carolina and Georgia made this a condition of their joining the Union. Both Jefferson and Washington hoped that slavery would soon die out, which it might have done if the invention of the cotton gin had not made cotton such a profitable crop that slavery (however wasteful in the long run) seemed essential to growing it. The United States forbade the importation of slaves in 1808, and Britain, after long debate, effectively ended her slave trade in 1811. Although the trade continued for a time in Latin America, Argentina had the foresight to decree that slaves' children born after 1813 should be free. But when the northern United States abolished slavery following Vermont in 1777, the "peculiar institution" merely gravitated to the South, where slaves were the main investment for the vast plantations, and breeding them became profitable after imports ceased to come from Africa. In 1852 passion overcame reason when Harriet Beecher Stowe published *Uncle Tom's Cabin* as a disguised tract against the 1850 law that allowed the pursuit of fugitive slaves into free states (ill. 158). Some years later, Lincoln summed up the effect of this famous novel when he greeted Mrs. Stowe by saying: "So you're the little woman who made the book that made this great war."

*Civil War Prints*

The Civil War of 1861–1865 produced the first large lot of photographs of any national conflict and a corresponding quantity of illustrations in periodicals, which are too close to the mainsheam of art to include in this book. The pictorial poster still lay so far in the future that the propaganda for recruiting used little more than plain type (ill. 159). The war produced a great deal of political cartooning by draftsmen as uninspired as the designer of the satire on the Bank of the United States (ill. 59). Although the North had the heavy preponderance of artistic and industrial skills, one of the very few cartoonists with a naive popular appeal worked for the Southern side. This was Adalbert Volck, an Augsburger, born in 1828 and trained in painting and sculpture at Nuremberg and Munich. He had escaped from Germany during the political troubles of 1848. After trying life in California and St. Louis, he settled in Baltimore, where he supported himself as a dentist while continuing to paint and model on the side. During the war he published a set of *Confederate War Etchings* in the outline manner popularized by Moritz Retzsch's illustrations for *Faust*, published in Dresden in 1816. His satire of Lincoln as a fugitive slave in a freight car (ill. 161) is perhaps the only political cartoon of the time that we can still look at with interest. The war also produced many pretty red-white-and-blue emblems of patriotism printed in the North on envelopes for letters to cheer soldiers at the front. Surprisingly few dramatic big lithographs were printed at the time (ill. 163), though many retrospective ones appeared in the 1880s and '90s when the by then middle-aged veterans published their war memoirs.

*Aftermath of the War*

The Civil War built up profiteer fortunes and a drive of energy that exploded into civilian action as soon as peace allowed it. The first great task was a project that had been discussed for twenty years, and had been begun while the war was still going on—the construction of a railway some three thousand miles (4,800 kilometers) from coast to coast. This engineering feat, which ranks with the Simplon Tunnel and the Suez Canal, was completed in May 1865, one month after the war's end. The work drove at backbreaking speed in dread lest the East and West might divide as the North and South had just finished dividing. An east-west railway had become necessary when the Southern army blockaded the north-south artery of the Mississippi River. The massive traffic that once had flowed on the river now turned forever to the new rails that led to both oceans. To finance the investment in laying rails across the wide plains and over the Rocky Mountains, the government granted the railway builders vast tracts of virgin lands on each side of the tracks. When the seaboard states were slow in sending people to buy these lands, the railway agents took alluring brochures to Scandinavia and Germany. Families and whole villages came by shiploads to regroup on the plains in hamlets and townships that rapidly grew into great cities, many of which are characterized to this day by the Lutheran faith of their origin.

The traffic to the new cities and the fruitful wheatlands enriched the railways until they dominated business during the disorders of reconstruction after the war. A few unscrupulous adventurers fought to possess the new prize. The sordid struggle became titanic enough to trouble the stock exchanges of Europe when Commodore Cornelius Vanderbilt had consolidated various short railways into a continuous line from New York to Buffalo on Lake Erie and then tried to buy out his competitor, the Erie Railroad. The directors of the Erie, James Fisk, Daniel Drew, and Jay Gould, flooded the market with unauthorized shares of stock that Vanderbilt recklessly bought in (ill. 162). Then the three swindlers ran with six million dollars of the Erie's money across the New York State boundary to barricade themselves in a New Jersey hotel. From there they bribed the New York State legislature to legalize the fraudulent issue of stock. When Fisk was murdered in 1872 in a quarrel over one of his mistresses, he had milked the Erie Railroad so effectively that it could pay no dividends for over sixty years. But in 1873 Vanderbilt emerged as the ultimate victor by buying tracks that took his lines from New York all the way to Chicago, thus becoming the master of one of the busiest transportation systems of the world.

## Sporting Prints

James Fisk had started his career of swindling by working in a circus. Quite understandably, he and other neck-or-nothing gamblers spent their new money on spectator sports that they organized on an almost Roman scale. In a smaller way, American sports had already entered the international scene when the Virginian Negro Molyneux boxed with Cribbs in England in 1811, and the yacht *America* raced the Royal Yacht Squadron at Cowes in 1851 (ill. 105).

Before the Civil War most sports had been intimate local events that were often illegal, such as cockfights and "rat worries" (ill. 165). The white man had learned his hunting from the Indians—how to set traps for foxes, mink, and beavers and to dress in furs that did not alarm animals, how to angle for fish in the winter through holes cut in the ice, and to spear fish at night by luring them with a torch held in an Indian canoe, how to play lacrosse, and to shoot with bow and arrows, which had been forgotten in Europe. The British gentleman's sport of shooting became the American's often desperate chance for survival. Since powder and bullets were scarce, many a hunter had to bag his supper with one shot, and when he had bullets to waste for sport, he shot at a turkey whose head bobbed up erratically behind a wall. Such exercises trained the unsoldierly but deadly marksmen who fought so effectively in the Revolution. We still remember our ancestors' skill when we say that a thing is "as sure as shooting."

In 1826 the introduction of English cartridges simplified loading guns and made shooting into a gentleman's sport. Americans began to shoot rail and other marsh birds from flat-bottomed boats poled over the marsh grass at high tide (ill. 164). When "pushing for rail" a hunter had to remember not to let the falling tide strand him for a sloshy tramp home.

American women were slow to take part in sports. The women who lived on farms or who adventured into the West had all they could do just to keep alive, and those in the Atlantic coastal cities shared the soft and sedentary life of the urban men. So it surprises one to see women of the 1880s playing billiards (ill. 166). Yet the game had been played by women at least since Shakespeare made Cleopatra say "Let's to billiards," and Mary Queen of Scots complained of being deprived of her billiard table in her prison castle. Another sport open to women was ice skating, which Dutch women must have transplanted from old Amsterdam to the new. Skating became possible the year around, and in places that never freeze, when roller skates were introduced from England in 1863. The craze spread

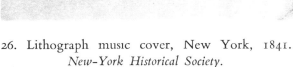

26. Lithograph music cover, New York, 1841.
*New-York Historical Society.*

27. Lithograph music cover, New York, 1840s.
*New-York Historical Society.*

to all major cities. San Francisco's rink had an immense hardwood floor (ill. 25) and five thousand pairs of skates to rent to skaters who often waltzed in full evening dress.

The master sport in Britain, as in British America, was certainly horse racing. About a year after the British seized New Amsterdam from the Dutch in 1664, the British commander laid out a racecourse on Long Island for annual spring and fall meets to be run for a silver cup. In time New York City and the southern states became the centers of horse racing. New York threw itself into the sport because it is the only northern city whose founders did not crave to establish a new Zion in the wilderness, but merely wanted, like good Dutchmen, to make money and enjoy it. Southerners took to horse racing because they rode in the saddle over trails too rough for carriages, and because they thought, like the British, that racing improves the breed of horses. Charleston, South Carolina, built a racetrack so famous that New Yorkers sailed there in special ships for the February meets, and Kentucky to this day holds races that the entire nation watches on television. Southern racing developed the fine horses

and horsemen that won cavalry victories for the South at the beginning of the Civil War.

New York built a series of grandstands that eventually seated nine thousand spectators, in addition to the tens of thousands who stood about (ill. 167). The betting that always goes with horses had made New England long ago reject classic saddle racing, though it accepted a different, and peculiarly American, variation of the sport whose origin is worth describing. After 1800, when roads improved, people gave up riding in the saddle for driving in carriages. Safer and lighter carriages stimulated drivers with fast teams to race each other on the spur of the moment, wherever they might be. When these offhand contests became more common, harness racing invaded the racetracks to become one of the most popular American sports (ill. 170), as trotters pulled light two-wheeled gigs. Some trotters became national heroes. In 1833 a rather unhandsome mare was foaled in Suffolk County, New York, and was named Lady Suffolk, but became famous as The Old Grey Mare. For fifteen years she kept the grit and stamina to win eighty-eight out of one hundred and thirty-eight races. So many people wanted to

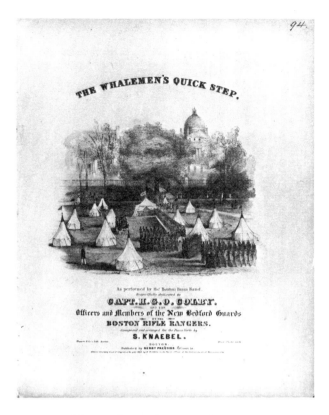

28. Lithograph music cover, Boston, 1842.
*New-York Historical Society.*

29. Lithograph music cover, Boston, 1848.
*New York, Metropolitan Museum of Art.*

see her in a riverside city that she had to be put on a boat that drifted slowly past the cheering crowds. Her death in 1854 saddened as many people as the death of any president. While only the rich could afford to own saddle horses in the North, every man who drove a cart felt that he was holdings the reins himself when he watched harness racing.

*Posters for Traveling Entertainments*

Shows of horsemanship played a large part in shaping the American version of the circus into a form quite different from the more or less settled circuses of Europe that play to city audiences in comparatively small permanent buildings. But no matter whether the circus is in a hall or an American tent, the size and form of the ring is the standard one established in 1768 when a British cavalryman, Philip Astley, discovered that centrifugal force enabled him to stand on his head on a horse's back if the horse kept running around a circle about forty-two feet (22 meters) in diameter. Trick riding quickly fascinated the British and then the Americans.

An American, Levi North, helped to found the American circus by turning fifty-five somersaults on a horse running around the standard-size ring. Exhibitions of athletic skill had already been popular at least as long ago as 1744 when a tightrope walker had delighted Society Hill in Philadelphia. New Yorkers were fascinated by the first elephant that walked on Broadway in 1796. The second elephant to come to the United States, called Old Bet, traveled around New England by night so that people would pay to see her in barns during the day until she came to Maine, where a farmer was so outraged at these ungodly goings-on that he shot her dead. For decades thereafter every traveling show took care to advertise itself as an uplifting and moral education. The American circus also absorbed the dried crocodiles, Pharaonic mummies and fake curiosities (ill. 33) that had been shown in country fairs. Fairground clowns and barkers then completed the circus.

Since no American city had a population like London or Paris that could support a resident circus, the American circus had to take to the road. At first the circus carts made a ring in the open air where people sat or stood as best they could, but by 1836

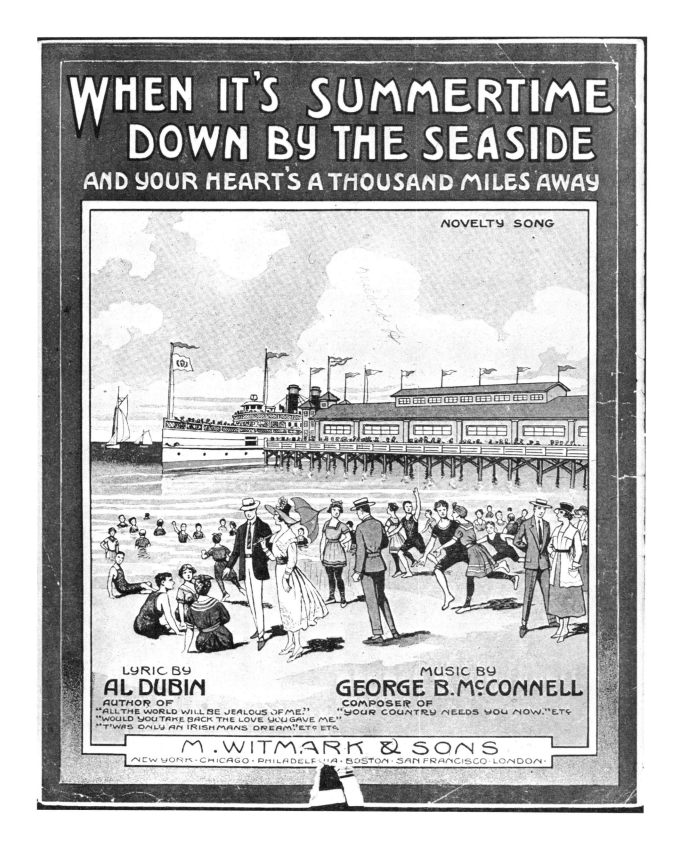

30. Sheet music cover, New York, about 1915.
*Woodrow Gelman Collection.*

The Church of The True Vine.

the old canvas fair booth had already been enlarged into the round tent—the Big Top—that ultimately seated up to ten thousand spectators. As soon as a good number of the short railway lines had been joined together in the 1850s, the circus loaded its ornate wagons onto flatcars in the order in which they would be driven off the end of the train for parading through the town. These wagons (ill. 168) were modeled on the seventeenth-century prints of allegorical chariots in baroque triumphs. A week or so before the arrival of the circus, an advance courier would paste gaudy posters on every conspicuous wall (ill. 174). The old circus tours aroused an excitement that is hard to imagine in our days of television. People came from faraway farms and villages long before dawn to watch the roustabouts wrestle with the huge tent, then they ran to the railway station to see the twenty or thirty gilded wagons file off the end of the train, and finally they paid their entrance into the big tent in the early afternoon.

The conditions that forced the American circus to travel also put the theatre on the road. Theatrical companies from London began playing in New York around 1750, and some later repertory companies managed to survive in one place by extremely hard work. In St. Louis during 1839 a company produced one hundred and fifty-seven different plays. Obviously no actor could be anything like letter perfect, and many must have gone on the stage without any rehearsal to "wing the part." The play must have been kept going by the steady reading of the prompter, as it was in the brilliantly inventive touring companies of Giovanni Grasso and Mimi Aguglia. After 1852 many troupes, called Tom Shows, toured with nothing but a dramatization of *Uncle Tom's Cabin*. After the Civil War the public began to demand melodramas with elaborate scenic effects such as locomotives running at the heroine tied to the tracks, dungeons filling with water to drown the handsome hero, or death leaps from viaducts (ill. 171). When producers drew crowds by publicizing highly paid stars, the various innovations increased costs until the run of the play had to be prolonged by tours that were advertised like the

41

circus by gaudy posters (ill. 175). Chromolithographic posters for spectacles had become a specialty of Currier & Ives in the 1880s (ill. 170). Since their posters mostly announced undifferentiated events like horse races, Currier & Ives could cut costs by printing a bright image of the general type of show and adding specific lettering as required. But such generalized posters did not suit most circuses and would not do at all for dramas. After about 1890, these newer specific posters were printed by specialist presses in Cincinnati, which was also the American headquarters for printing playing cards. The story of the designers of these posters has not yet been dug out of whatever may survive in the way of records of the printing firms. And American businesses have a way of junking all trace of their past.

### The Dime Novel

Young Americans have always been supplied with some equivalent of the drastic simplicities of melodrama, whether it be through Grimm's violent folk tales, the disasters so well deserved by Miss Patty Proud (ill. 3), or Davy Crockett's rough-and-tumble fights (ill. 21). For an adult audience Edgar Allan Poe perfected the detective story with *The Murders in the Rue Morgue* in 1843. These elements—the youth who conquers fame, fortune, and a princess, the moral example, and one man's clever campaign against evil—all combined in a typically American form of fiction known as the dime novel.

The actual name was invented by two brothers called Beadle, who grew up on a farm in upstate New York. Erastus Beadle, born in 1821, became interested in printing when he cut letters in wood to stamp bags of grain. He then learned all branches of book production while working for a printer in a nearby town, where his brother Irwin Beadle made a local success by publishing a *Dime Song Book*. In 1858 the brothers came to New York determined to rival the current expensive books with wide margins, elegant typography, and hard covers by adapting the format of the almanacs (ills. 21-23, 125) for huge editions of paperback booklets of songs, cookery recipes, and model letters priced at ten cents, or one dime. In June 1860, they published the first of about a thousand adventure stories in a series that they called Dime Novels. A year or so later, millions of these were selling to soldiers in the Northern camps of the Civil War and were being exchanged with Confederate soldiers in the rare moments of fraternizing. Though rival publishers entered the field as soon as the war was over, the Beadle books set the tone for the early dime novels, adventure stories laid among the Indians or during the struggle of the Revolution. In the 1870s the dime novel was deflected by the success of the detective stories written by Allan Pinkerton out of his own experiences. Pinkerton, born in 1819 as the son of a Glasgow police sergeant, became involved in the Scottish branch of the radical workers' Chartist movement and fled to Illinois in 1842. While working there for the Underground Railroad that smuggled runaway slaves, he broke up a gang of counterfeiters. In 1850 he became the first detective on the Chicago police force and started the first private detective agency to help the railroads solve train robberies. During the Civil War he spied in the South as part of the intelligence system that he organized for the Northern army. After a slight stroke kept him at home in 1869, he used his enforced leisure to write eighteen volumes based on his astonishing adventures. Thereafter no dime novel could ignore the daring youth who thwarts a villainous plot or two in the streets of Philadelphia, or on the steel girders of a New York building under construction (ill. 183), or dives for a ferryboat (ill. 179). Whatever the theme, the dime novel had to open with a startling statement such as "We will have the money, or she shall die," or else

"BANG!

"BANG!

"BANG!

"Three shots broke the still midnight."

So many writers dashed off these adventures at top speed that the Beadles published a code of rules for the manuscripts that they might consider purchasing for fifty or a hundred dollars:

> We prohibit all things offensive to good taste, in expression or incident—
> We prohibit what cannot be read with satisfaction by every right-minded person — old or young alike—
> We prohibit subjects or characters that carry an immoral *taint*—
> We require pronounced strength of plot and high dramatic interest of story—
> We require your best work—

Dime novels overflowed into all the English-speaking world as shilling shockers that brought Kit Carson, California Joe, Jesse James, the Bowery Boy, Deadwood Dick and his Calamity Jane as typical Americans to boys in Britain, South Africa,

ROPER'S GYMNASIUM.
874 MARKET STREET PHILADELPHIA.

32. Philadelphia gymnasium, about 1830. Lithograph by E. W. Clay.
*New York Public Library.*

and Australia. Italian boys knew these novels by reading *Nick Carter, il gran poliziotto americano* and *Buffalo Bill, l'eroe del Wild West*. After the First World War this immense production succumbed to the comics, the early Western movies, and the radio serials of "The Lone Ranger" and "The Green Hornet." Dime novels had the lure of the illicit for many a boy whose parents banished them from the house, feeling that so much entertainment must vitiate their high moral tone. They were read to shreds by boys who masked them inside copies of *Pilgrim's Progress* or Euclid's *Geometry* when they could not sneak away to the frank seclusion of the hayloft. Dime novels in good condition have become among the rarest of all nineteenth-century American books. This is a pity because the illustrators who drew their brightly colored covers gradually worked out of a routine romantic exaggeration into a brisk and shrewdly studied glimpse of contemporary life (ills. 177, 179, 183). In fact, the cover illustrations of these later dime novels look more "real" than the even more lurid pictures that pretended to represent

actual crimes in the *Police Gazette* (ills. 180–184). These superb confrontations of Virtue and Vice played their minor part in enticing readers away from the more obviously moral dime novels.

*The Comic Strip*

The really fatal rival of the dime novel was certainly the comic strip. Where the dime novel had only one picture on the cover, the comic strip told half, and sometimes all, of its story through pictures. Thus the comic strip could do more than the dime novel to reach the hundreds of thousands of immigrants who came out of non-English-speaking countries to the United States from about the 1880s until the restrictive immigration acts during the First World War. The basic idea of the comic strip—a continuous pictorial narrative—is almost as old as drawing itself. The comics got their present format from the aggressive newspaper editors of the English-speaking world, Alfred Harmsworth (later

Lord Northcliffe) and William Randolph Hearst. In 1890 young Harmsworth, then aged twenty-five, started two series of continuous funny pictures, set in black and white to capture the public for the cheapest newspapers. He "killed the penny dreadful with the ha'penny dreadfuller." Then in 1892 Hearst started a comic strip of animals in San Francisco, but it was not until five years later that he got his first great inspiration from Wilhelm Busch's immortal bad boys *Max und Moritz*, published in 1858. Hearst commissioned Rudolph Dirks to naturalize them as the Katzenjammer Kids in a series that was to run for over seventy years. All of these early American comics were printed in color as full or half-page supplements to Sunday papers. The first black-and-white single-strip daily comic in the United States was Bud Fisher's Mutt and Jeff, which started in 1908 in San Francisco and was soon bought by Hearst for as long a run as the Katzenjammer Kids. The next great innovation came when Harold R. Foster adapted Edgar Rice Burroughs's novel *Tarzan* for the first adventure story in comic form. Foster also introduced the magazine illustrator's technique of slashing black-and-white brushwork with realistic anatomical modeling. Heretofore the figures had been flat marionettes that made their effect by their lively outline against blank backgrounds in the small space left under the continuous cloud formation of speaking balloons. The 1930s learned from the movies to vary the sequence of pictures with occasional close-ups and unexpected camera angles. Comics began to spread enormously when they were syndicated for nationwide circulation in 1913, so that a popular series like Blondie appeared in over 1,300 newspapers. Almost every paper prints a wide selection of comics because of differences in reader preference. The comics echo in the background of our minds the way ballads echoed in the ages before printing.

Although Mutt and Jeff appeared in book form in 1911, it was not until the 1930s that the comic books were published in quantity. Though most of them reprinted newspaper comics, they soon developed many different forms. Pornography found an ideal presentation until the publishers voluntarily, but not permanently, censored themselves in 1954. Educators used the comic book to teach useful skills, to dramatize the latest developments in science, and to digest great works of literature such as *Les Misérables*, *Gulliver's Travels*, *Don Quixote*, and the Bible. Many an American boy has first met Samson bringing down the jawbone of an ass that trails a meteor tail of WHAM!!! Who shall say that this is not a perfectly good introduction to Holy Writ? Is it not the modern equivalent to the Bibles in stone carved for the illiterate on medieval cathedral doors? Comic books reached their heyday when the soldiers of the Second World War devoured them by the hundred thousand the way Civil War soldiers had devoured dime novels.

Some of the early comics were the most imaginative. When Gertrude Stein gave the Katzenjammer Kids to Picasso their expressive shorthand drawing inspired his impudence the way ragtime had inspired Debussy. Many early strips came out of pure introspective fantasy, like the Wigglemuch series by Herbert Crowley (ill. 34). Crowley was born near London in 1873. Though he studied singing in Paris, he could never bring himself to face an audience. Then, while working in a mine, he discovered that he could draw. His late-found career took him eventually to the *New York Herald*, where he drew the Wigglemuch from about 1910 to 1914. In his solitary imagination, this creature with no legs on its far side became more actual than anybody he met on the street. Crowley could tell you exactly when it slept, what it did and did not eat, how it laughed, and that it whistled like you and me. His patient, meticulously factual fantasies were sometimes printed on the same page of the *Herald* with Winsor McCay's intricate dreams.

Winsor McCay was one of the true geniuses of the comics. Born in 1869, the son of a Michigan lumber-mill owner, he went in his later teens to Chicago, where he lived with Jules Guerin, a mural painter from St. Louis, who was three years older than McCay and probably passed on some art-school training. Guerin might even have given McCay his sense of the monumental and his pattern that lies flat on the page. At seventeen McCay began to earn his living by advertising the coming arrival of a traveling circus as he decorated any large walls with freehand paintings of bearded ladies, sword swallowers, fire-eaters, trapeze artists, and wild beasts. While he was doing this in Cincinnati, his skill attracted the attention of the editor of the *Times-Star*, who hired him in 1888 to illustrate the newspaper with drawings of weddings, fires, accidents, and murders. When his work became known in New York he joined the *New York Herald* in 1903, where he began to draw the dreams of his little son, Winsor, Jr., in a Sunday supplement called Little Nemo (Little Nobody) in Slumberland (ill. 185). This captivated so many people that it was made into a musical play in 1906. McCay's command of hand enabled him to invent with unbelievable abundance. As if his

# THE GREATEST
# NATURAL CURIOSITY
## In the known World!

The above Groupe was found petrified in the southern part of South America, by Mr. Abel Gordon, of England, and is the most marvellous and wonderful curiosity that man ever beheld. The imagination cannot picture, nor words describe the sublime effect that a view of it produces.

## THE GROUPE CONSISTS OF A

# HORSE & ITS INDIAN RIDER,
### WITH AN
# ENORMOUS SERPENT
## COILED AROUND THEM !

The Serpent must have been poisoned by a poisoned shaft, thrust into it by the Indian in his struggle of defence, and is broken off. The whole is in a most perfect petrified state of preservation : the size of the serpent is so enormous as to appear incredible, being

## 40 feet long and about 3 in circumference.

☞ It is now on exhibition, for a short time, previous to taking it to Europe, at the NEW YORK SOCIETY LIBRARY LECTURE ROOM,

## ☞ NO. 348 BROADWAY,
### Price of ADMISSION ONLY 25 CENTS,
so as to give every one an opportunity to see it, and no one should fail to improve it.

### Doors open from 9 in the morning until 10 at night.

N. B. This specimen was found about 100 miles east of the Volcano of Chillan, and about six hundred West by South from the port of Buenos Ayres, by Mr. Gordon. While there, the Native Indians gave him information of its existence, and appeared to have a superstitious fear of molesting it. It was obtained with great difficulty from a deep ravine or cave, overhung by rugged cliffs of limestone.

Congress Printing House, (J. E. Farwell & Co.) printers, 32 Congress st.

33. Wood-engraved poster, New York, 1840s.
*New-York Historical Society.*

Sunday stint were not enough, he also drew a week-day black-and-white strip of the Dreams of a Rarebit Fiend, thus becoming the first man to draw, all by himself, a complete comic feature every single day. Then in 1909, when his son picked up a flip book in the street, McCay turned Little Nemo into the first animated cartoon with four thousand drawings. He regarded this as a mere experiment for the first animation that made a sensation with the public. This was Gertie the Dinosaur, at whose showings McCay used to appear in person to supply dialogue for the film: "Here, Gertie, here's an apple for you. Come on, eat it out of my hand, that's a good girl. There we go. Did it taste good?"—and so on. In the newspaper office he would sometimes note intended colors on the margins of his India ink drawings, but most of the delicate tints were supplied by a tasteful printer. When this printer died, the colors became more garish. McCay had taught himself enough anatomy to draw figures in any position without a model, and he mastered perspective as absolutely as the great Italian stage designers of the baroque. Had he been born in Italy in 1669 instead of the United States in 1869, he would have startled opera audiences in princely theatres with worlds of endless illusion. As it was, he gave the same poetic release to millions of Americans cooped up in little white frame houses. Just as the baroque stage designers had dazzled the absolute monarchs with palaces that even they were not able to build in actual stone, so McCay showed Americans the incredible cities that were not to arise in actual steel until after he died in 1934.

## Argentina and Brazil

Goya's solitary achievement in prints distracts one from the fact that Spain and Portugal actually lagged far behind the rest of Europe and so had little impulse to send to Latin-American printmaking. The great Latin-American cities—Havana, Mexico City, Rio de Janeiro, Lima, Buenos Aires— were pictured in considerable detail in handsome wide lithographs that were often published in Paris, and in aquatints published in London, but there seems to have been little printmaking at home except in Mexico. While Latin Americans have collected and described their early books, only the Mexicans have done very much either way about their early prints. The strong French influence that directs the architecture of Buenos Aires probably also introduced lithography at about the same time that Pendleton in Boston imported his French printer in 1826. A set of pen-drawn lithographs issued at Buenos Aires in 1833/1834 bears two French-sounding names, C. H. Bade as the printer, and as draftsman H. Moulin, who might be a certain Sainte Marie Ludovic Hardouin Hippolyte Moulin who showed chromolithographs in the Paris salons in 1848 to 1879. Most of these Customs and Costumes of the Province of Buenos Aires (Trajes y Costumbres de la Provincia de Buenos Aires) are routine satires of women in crinolines so wide that they block traffic, and combs so high that they scrape the lintels of doors. One of the set, however, allows a sympathetic glimpse into the indolent seclusion of a lady of Buenos Aires, a porteña, as she sips maté through a silver straw brought to her by a little black page boy (ill. 186).

France may have played a smaller part in introducing lithography into Brazil. Our illustration of a German trade fair, on the outskirts of Porto Alegre (ill. 187) is signed by B. Hugo as draftsman, which sounds French, and E. Wiedemann as the lithographic printer. Neither of these names appears in published lists of artists, but Wiedemann, while it could be Alsatian, is more probably as German as the fair that he drew with such factual bleakness.

## Mexico Again

Ever since at least 1570 Mexicans have made prints with vigor enough to need only a very occasional nudge from outside. Eighteenth-century engravers turned out a copious commercial line of Virgins of Guadalupe, Virgins of Solitude, Flagellations, and Crucifixions. Though these stiff little icons were certainly engraved with unquestioning devotion for an equally devout public, it takes more than sincerity to make an impact on the beholder. Like so much folk art, the Mexican holy images behave as the pretty flowers that one finds in the woods and takes home only to see them droop and fade away. After about the 1830s, lithographic presses took on the production of holy images, and added satires of manners and politics in periodicals patterned on La Caricature, started in Paris in 1831. Cartooning found an ideal climate in Mexico that still throbs from the shock of the encounter between the Aztec and the Spaniard when, for the only time in the world, two equally intricate civilizations clashed head on with no prior inkling of each other. The endemic turmoil of Mexico was aggravated by the imposition of Maximilian as emperor in 1864 and was then accelerated to frenzy by his execution in 1867. The country did not begin

34. Comic strip by Herbert Crowley, New York, 1910.
*New York, Metropolitan Museum of Art, gift of Mrs. Herbert Crowley.*

to settle down until the 1920s. In 1852, as these long troubles were about to begin, an Indian boy, José Guadalupe Posada, the son of a baker, was born in the central Mexican town of Aguascalientes (Hot Springs). While still a child he worked at pottery for an uncle, and then helped a schoolteacher brother by instructing his pupils in drawing. At fifteen, a census listed him as a painter, though none of his paintings have been identified. The next year he began to lithograph cigar-box labels, diplomas, letterheads, and illustrations for a local printer who had studied at the Aguascalientes Academy of Fine Arts and must have passed on the rudiments of factual rendering, as well as the techniques of lithography and woodcutting. By 1871 Posada was already lithographing neat satires for the local paper *El Jicote* (*The Hornet*), and in 1876 he bought his employer's Hoe press with six lithographic stones, which had been moved to the busier town of Leon de los Aldamas. Then in 1888 a spring flood drowned Leon, and Posada left for Mexico City for the rest of his life.

A year or so after settling in the capital, he began a lifelong association with Mexico's leading publisher of popular literature, Antonio Vinegas Arroyo, who had begun in 1880 to do for Mexico what the Beadle brothers' dime publications had done in 1860 for the United States. Vinegas Arroyo's advertisement covers the range of subjects that Posada was called on to illustrate: "This year's songs, collections of compliments, magic tricks, riddles, parlor games, booklets on cooking, candy and pastry making, toasts, rhymes for jokers, patriotic speeches, plays for children or puppets, entertaining stories; The New Oracle, or The Book of the Future; How to tell Fortunes with Cards; The New Mexican Fortune Teller; Black and White Magic, or The Book of Sorcerers." Vinegas Arroyo also published broadsides on orange, green, or raspberry tissue paper with poems for night watchmen to give to their clients on New Year's Day as a reminder to pay them, with funny ballads, with details of yesterday's murder or suicide, and with so many executions under Porfirio Diaz's dictatorship that a typical cut of a firing squad was kept ready printed for hastily dubbing in the latest victim's end (ill. 35). Until his

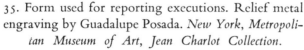

35. Form used for reporting executions. Relief metal engraving by Guadalupe Posada. *New York, Metropolitan Museum of Art, Jean Charlot Collection.*

36. *42 Riddles,* book cover by Guadalupe Posada. *New York, Metropolitan Museum of Art, Jean Charlot Collection.*

death in 1913 Posada worked for Vinegas Arroyo from his own shop in the sanguinary turbulence of the slums, where his window glass was patched with paper, his workroom was stacked helter-skelter with thousands of engraved blocks, and his narrow street front barely squeezed in the huge letters that advertised

## ILLUSTRATIONS FOR PERIODICALS, BOOKS AND ANNOUNCEMENTS

He had himself photographed lounging in the doorway—a big man of sedentary corpulence, in a wrinkled middle-class suit, with the flush, compact features, and the prominent eyes of the colossal stone heads that the Olmecs had carved southeast of his birthplace two thousand years before.

When Posada first arrived in the capital he drew

almost his last lithographs for a periodical in 1888 and 1889. Then, perhaps to fit in with Vinegas Arroyo's way of illustrating his cheap little books, he specialized in various kinds of relief blocks. He often used the process line block, invented in Paris in the 1870s, by which zinc is marked with lines of a material that resists acid. These protected lines are then left in relief when acid eats down the surrounding naked metal. The resulting relief block looks like a rubber stamp, and can be printed in the same press and at the same time as type, instead of requiring a special press like the lithographic stone. In today's books and magazines the lines of a pen drawing are photographicaly converted into acid-proof lines on the zinc. But since this requires a special camera and ultraviolet light, Posada tended after about 1891 to speed up and simplify the process so that it could all be done in his modest workshop by drawing directly on the zinc with a pen dipped in etcher's stopping-out varnish. His years of rendering precisely and factually on the lithographic stone had

37. Naughty Josephina Lara. Relief metal cut by Guadalupe Posada.
*New York, Metropolitan Museum of Art, Jean Charlot Collection.*

trained him to such a command of hand that he was able to juggle the line block's ragged-edged, syrupy line for a delicate vividness of expression (ill. 36). Posada also used gravers and gouges to scoop white lines in buttery type metal, often saving time with a multiple tool that cuts several parallel white lines at one stroke (ill. 35). These summary relief processes that admit no fine detail thereby force a shorthand simplification that challenged Posada to his greatest achievements. He visualized his intended image so exactly that he made no preliminary drawing to guide him before attacking the relief block. One day, as he was discussing a commission with a new client, he picked up a little block and began to make a few passes at it with a tool, now and then glancing at the visitor as they talked. Presently he went to his press and printed an unforgettable summation of his new friend.

When Posada left the provinces for the capital, he left small-town gentility for the volcano of the overcrowded city. He plunged headlong into his new neighborhood of rape, murder, and suicide with no shyness, no false modesty, or inhibitions to check his grand abandon to life's drama. Everywhere around him he saw, not tragedy, but passion; not death, but life. His many skeletons and skulls (*calaveras*) do not seem morbid in Mexico, where images of death have been a part of life since Aztec times (ills. 193, 194). Halloween is as much a feast for Mexican children as it is for children in the United States. With a sanguinary hilarity, Mexican children disguise themselves as ghosts and skeletons, and eat sugar-candy skulls with tinsel eye sockets, and a sweetheart's name dribbled in bright icing across the forehead.

Out of the volcano of his neighbors' lives Posada drew an energy that, after his death, was to stir Mexican painters of the 1920s and 1930s into becoming the sparkling center of all the Americas. Diego Rivera called Posada the "boiler" that drove art in Mexico. This reverses the usual direction of influence, whereby "high" art tends to rusticate into folk art,

49

just as court fashions fossilize into peasant costumes. But by the sheer force of his personality Posada became the only folk artist to animate a whole school of "high" art.

Posada is the one true genius among the many strong personalities that mark American popular printmaking, especially in the comics. In this the Americas resemble sixteenth-century Germany or eighteenth-century England rather than Italy, France, or Spain, where popular prints tended to be made in shops by anonymous artisans. North America in particular provided the unique adventures of subduing the wilderness and tapping—even recklessly exhausting—natural resources for the creation of giant industries. These two explorations stimulated an unusually varied popular art.

PLATES

38. The port of Philadelphia. Woodcut, Philadelphia 1808. *Princeton University Library, gift of Sinclair Hamilton.* ▷

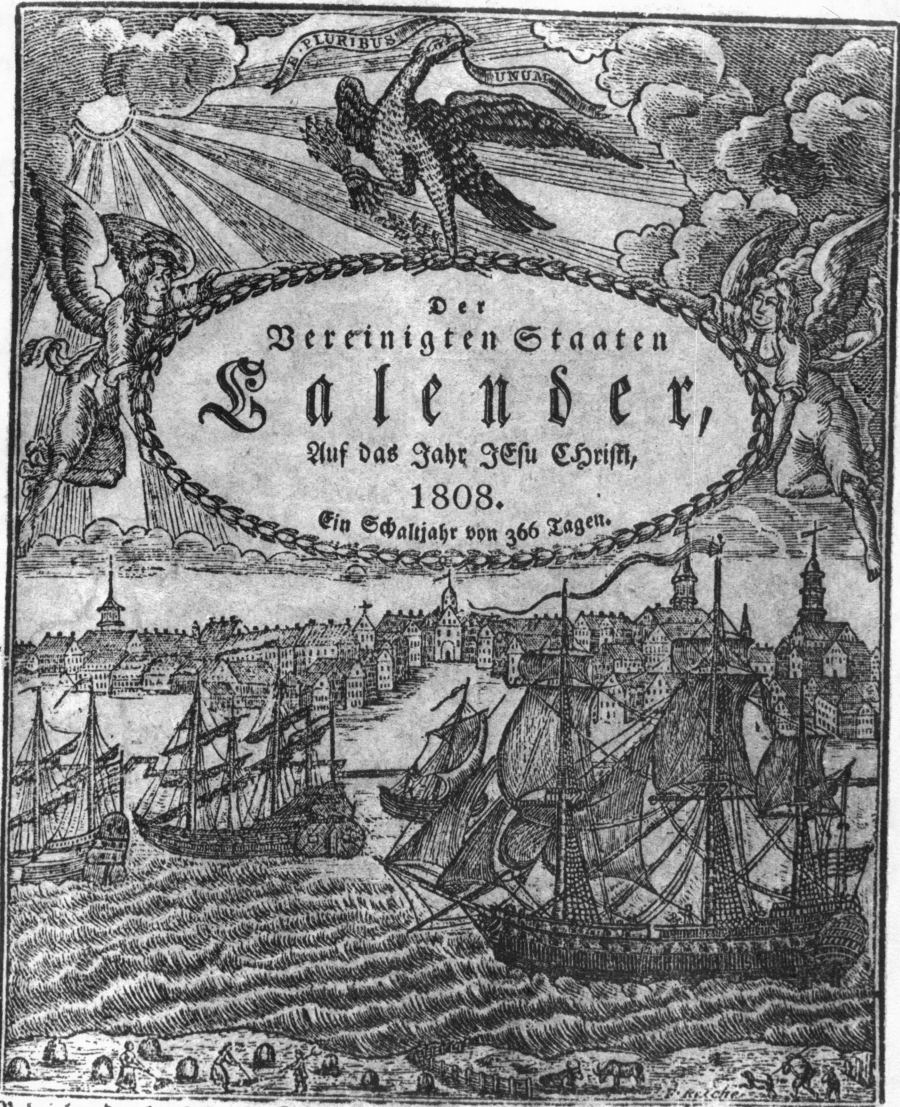

E. PLURIBUS UNUM

Der
Vereinigten Staaten
Calender,
Auf das Jahr JEsu Christi,
1808.
Ein Schaltjahr von 366 Tagen.

Philadelphia: Gedruckt bey Johann Geyer, No. 122. in der Dritten, vier Thüren oberhalb der Rees-straße.

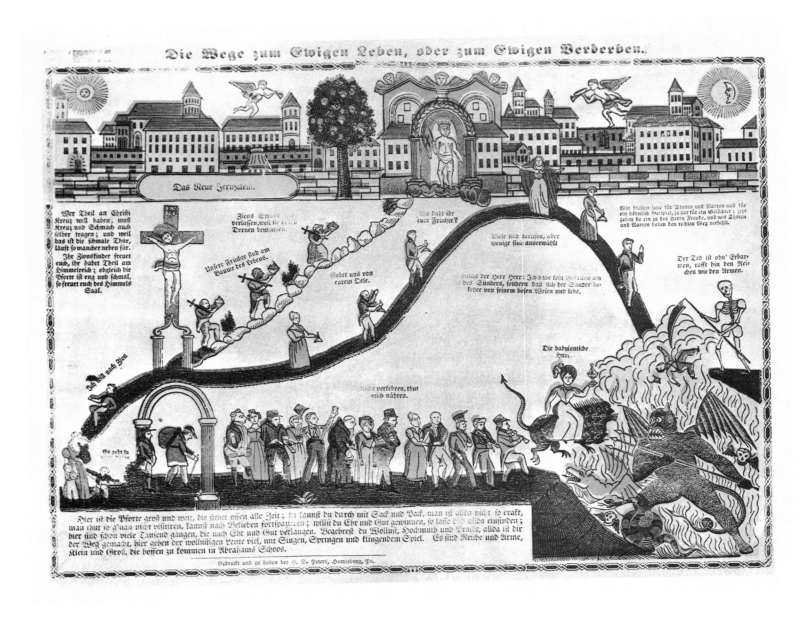

39. The roads to Hell and to Heaven. Stencil-colored woodcut, Harrisburg, Pennsylvania, 1830s.
*New-York Historical Society.*

40. Hand colored woodcut, Pennsylvania, 1800–25.
*New-York Historical Society.*

41 Stencil-colored woodcut, Reading, Pennsylvania, 1800–25.
*New-York Historical Society.*

EL Efcudo de Armas de efte Imperio
De hijo de Aguila Real bien te acredita
Quando anciofo te fube al Emisferio
En que tu aguda vifta no palpita.
Con llegar á fubirte hafta el Hefperio
Pues tu alma mas allá fe depofita.
Llore pues con razon el Tenoxthlino
Pues que le falta vn Sol tan Peregrino.

42. Juan de Zumárraga: *Doctrina Breve*, Mexico, Juan Ocharte, 1543.
*New York, Hispanic Society of America.*

43. Allegory of Charles II of Spain. Engraving in Augustín de Mora:
*El Sol Eclypsado*, Mexico, Guillena, 1701.
*New York, Metropolitan Museum of Art.*

44. Catafalque of Philip IV in the Cathedral, Mexico City. Engraving in Isidro Sariñana: *Llanto del Occidente*, Mexico, Calderón, 1666. ▷
*New York, Metropolitan Museum of Art.*

Estas cuētas sō sincuēta. En valor e yficacia, El peccador q̃ os
reza, Jamas le faltara gracia. En meyico ē casa de. P̃. Ocharte 1571,

Mr. Richard Mather.

46. Richard Mather. Woodcut by John Foster, Boston, about 1670.
*Princeton University Library, gift of Frank Jewett Mather.*

◁ 45. The Virgin of the Rosary. Stencil-colored woodcut by Juan Ortiz, Mexico, 1571. *Mexico, Archivo Nacional.*

"Come Patty, she said,
"My good little maid;
"Come; let me have all things in order;
"Move quickly we must,
"So, you make the crust,
"And mind, and crimp nicely the border."

INDUSTRY.

47. Wood-engraved book illustration by John Warner Barber, New Haven, 1840s.
*New York, Metropolitan Museum of Art.*

48. Hand-colored etching in *History of little Jackey Horner*, Baltimore, about 1820.
*New York, Metropolitan Museum of Art, gift of Lincoln Kirstein.*

**DREAMER.**

Behold! within these mystic pages lie,
The hidden things of dark futurity.

THE WISE & FOOLISH PURCHASES.

49. Wood engraving in *The Dream Book*, Philadelphia, 1835. New York, Metropolitan Museum of Art, gift of Harry F. Harris.

50. Wood engraving in *Gift for Young Friends*, New York, 1848. *New York, Metropolitan Museum of Art, gift of William M. Ivins, Jr.*

The BLOODY MASSACRE perpetrated in King—ſ—Street BOSTON on March 5th 1770 by a party of the 29th REGt

BUTCHER'S HALL

Engrav'd Printed & Sold by PAUL REVERE BOSTON

Unhappy Boſton! ſee thy Sons deplore,
Thy hallow'd Walks beſmear'd with guiltleſs Gore:
While faithleſs P—n and his ſavage Bands,
With murd'rous Rancour ſtretch their bloody Hands;
Like fierce Barbarians grinning o'er their Prey,
Approve the Carnage, and enjoy the Day.

If ſcalding drops from Rage from Anguiſh Wrung,
If ſpeechleſs Sorrows lab'ring for a Tongue,
Or if a weeping World can ought appeaſe
The plaintive Ghoſts of Victims ſuch as theſe;
The Patriot's copious Tears for each are ſhed,
A glorious Tribute which embalms the Dead.

But know, Fate ſummons to that awful Goal,
Where Juſtice ſtrips the Murd'rer of his Soul:
Should venal C—ts the ſcandal of the Land,
Snatch the relentleſs Villain from her Hand,
Keen Execrations on this Plate inſcrib'd,
Shall reach a Judge who never can be brib'd.

The unhappy Sufferers were Meſſrs Saml Gray, Saml Maverick, Jams Caldwell, Crispus Attucks & Patk Carr
Reproduced 1954 Killed. Six wounded; two of them (Christr Monk & John Clark) Mortally

51. The Boston Massacre, 1770. Engraving by Paul Revere. *New York, Metropolitan Museum of Art.*

Place II. A View of the Town of Concord.

1 Companies of the Regulars marching into Concord.
2 Companies of Regulars drawn up in order.
3 A Detachment destroying the Provincial Stores.

4 & 5 Colonel Smith & Major Pitcairn viewing the Provincials
who were mustering on an East Hill in Concord.
6 The Townhouse. 7 The Meetinghouse.

A. Doolittle. Sculp.

52. The Battle of Lexington and Concord, 19 April, 1775. Engraved by Amos Doolittle after Ralph Earl, New Haven, 1775.
*New York Public Library.*

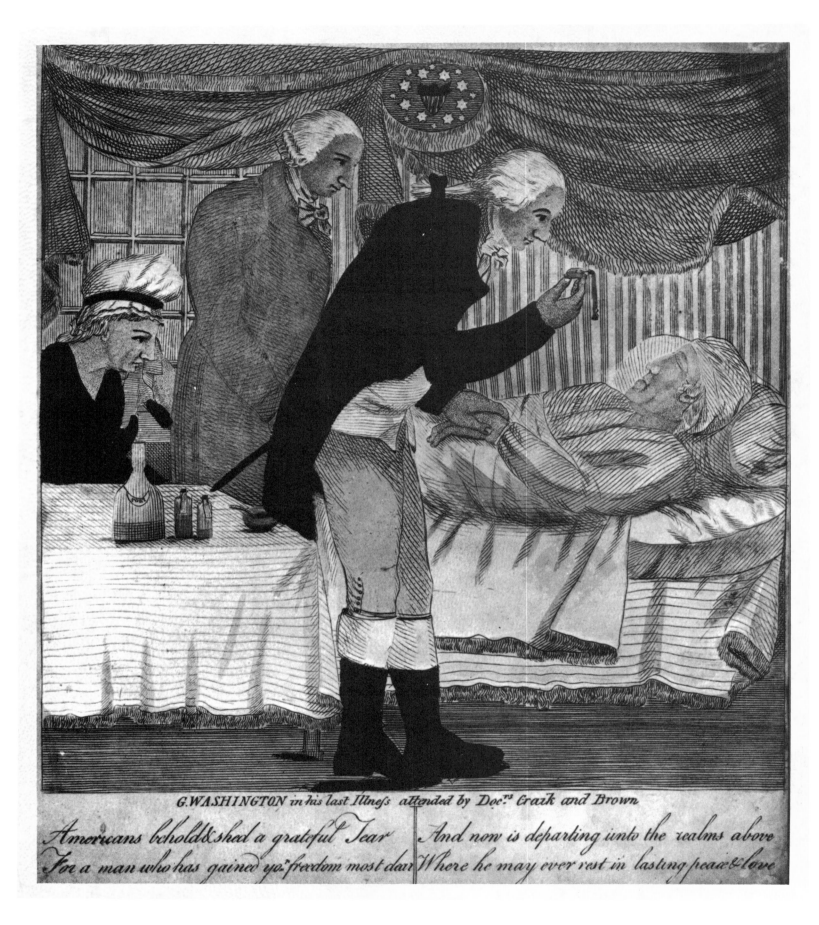

G.WASHINGTON *in his last Illness attended by Doc.ʳˢ Craik and Brown*

*Americans behold & shed a grateful Tear*      *And now is departing unto the realms above*
*For a man who has gained yoᵘ freedom most dear*   *Where he may ever rest in lasting peace & love*

53. The death of George Washington, 1799. Anonymous engraving.
*New-York Historical Society, Irving S. Olds Collection.*

54. Counterfeiter in the Pillory. Metal cut, Boston, 1767. *Pennsylvania Historical Society.* ▷

# A few LINES on
# Magnus Mode, Richard Hodges & J. Newington Clark.
### Who are Sentenc'd to stand one Hour in the
# Pillory at Charlestown;
To have one of their EARS cut off, and to be Whipped 20 Stripes at the public Whipping-Post, for making and passing Counterfeit DOLLARS, &c.

BEHOLD the villains rais'd on high !
(The *Post* they've got attracts the eye :)
Both Jews and Gentiles all appear
To see them stand exalted here ;
Both rich and poor, both young and old,
The dirty slut, the common scold :
What multitudes do them surround,
Many as bad as can be found.
And to encrease their sad disgrace,
Throw rotten eggs into their face,
And pelt them sore with dirt and stones,
Nay, if they could would break their bones.
Their malice to such height arise,
Who knows but they'll put out their eyes :
But pray consider what you do
While thus expos'd to public view.
Justice has often done its part,
And made the guilty rebels smart ;
But they went on did still rebel,
And seem'd to storm the gates of hell.
To no good counsel would they hear ;
But now each one must loose an EAR,

And they although against their will
Are forc'd to chew this bitter pill ;
And this day brings the villains hence
To suffer for their late offence ;
They on th' Pillory stand in view :
A warning firs to me and you !
The drunkards song, the harlots scorn,
Reproach of some as yet unborn.
But now the *Post* they're forc'd to hug,
But loath to take that nauseous drug
Which brings the blood from out their veins,
And marks their back with purple stains.
From their disgrace, now warning take,
And never do your ruin make
By stealing, or unlawful ways ;
(If you would live out all your days)
But keep secure from Theft and Pride ;
Strive to have virtue on your side.
Despise the harlot's flattering airs,
And hate her ways, avoid her snares ;
Keep clear from Sin of every kind,
And then you'll have true peace of Mind.

55. Canal and towpath. Lithograph by August Köllner in *Common Sights in Town and Country*, Philadelphia, about 1850.
*New York, Metropolitan Museum of Art, Dick Fund.*

56. Castle Garden Concert Hall, New York. Color woodcut hatbox covering, Boston (?), 1830s. *New York, Metropolitan Museum of Art.*

57. South Carolina bank notes. Metal relief prints, 1776.
*New York, Metropolitan Museum of Art.*

58. A business office, engraved by Alexander Lawson, Philadelphia, about 1798. *New-York Historical Society, Bella C. Landauer Collection.* ▷

A MERCHANTS COUNTING HOUSE

Publish'd by T. Dobson south 2 street Philad.

**GENERAL JACKSON SLAYING THE MANY HEADED MONSTER.**

59. Andrew Jackson destroying the Bank of the United States. Lithograph, New York, 1828. *New-York Historical Society.*

60. Book and stationery store. Engraving, Boston, about 1820.
*New-York Historical Society, Bella C. Landauer Collection.*

61. Lithograph trade card, New York, 1830s. *New-York Historical Society, Bella C. Landauer Collection.*

62. Lithograph trade card, New York, 1830s.
*New York, Metropolitan Museum of Art.*

63. Wood-engraved advertisement, Philadelphia, 1830s.
*New-York Historical Society.*

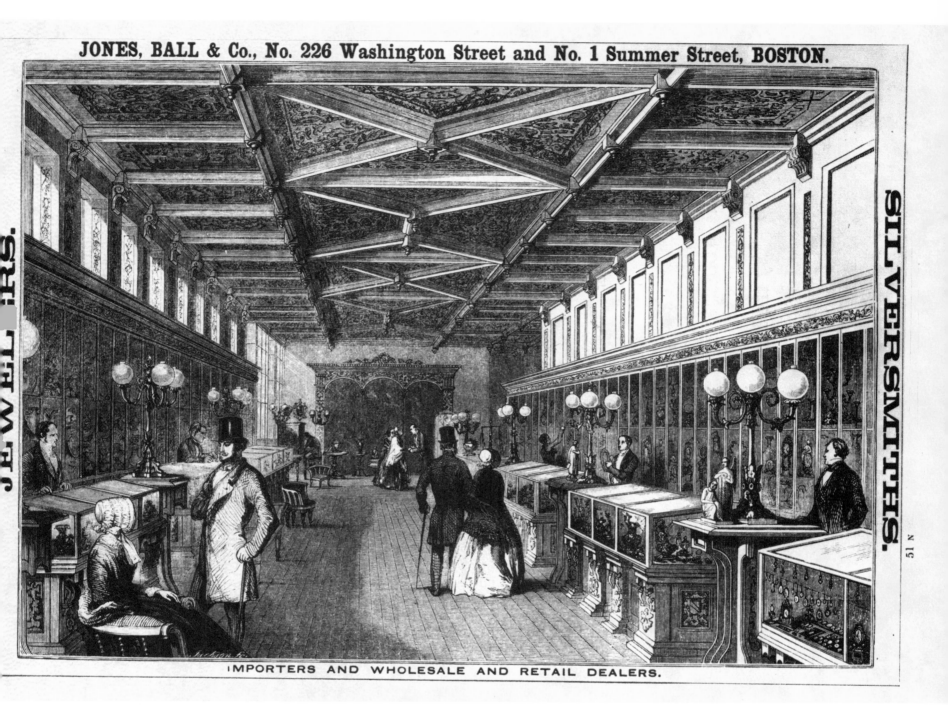

IMPORTERS AND WHOLESALE AND RETAIL DEALERS.

64. Wood-engraved advertisement, Boston, 1856. *New-York Historical Society, Bella C. Landauer Collection.*

WILLIAM GALE JR. & CO.

BROWN & SPAULDING.

Sterling Silver and Plated Ware.

Fine Jewelry, Bronzes and Fancy Goods.

572 & 574 Broadway.

568 & 570

New York City.

65. Jewelry and silverware store. Lithograph, New York,
about 1860. *New-York Historical Society.*

66. Chromolithograph poster, about 1910.
*New-York Historical Society, Bella C. Landauer Collection.*

67. Chromolithograph poster, Milwaukee, 1912.
*New-York Historical Society, Bella C. Landauer Collection.*

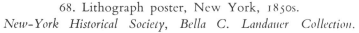

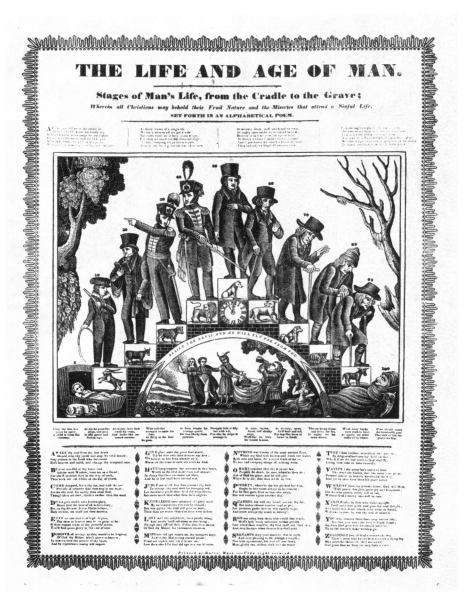

68. Lithograph poster, New York, 1850s.
*New-York Historical Society, Bella C. Landauer Collection.*

69. Wood engraved broadside, Barre, Massachusetts, 1840s.
*New-York Historical Society.*

70. Wood-engraved patent medicine advertisement, Albany, 1840s. *New-York Historical Society, Bella C. Landauer Collection.* ▷

# STOP, FRIEND!
## Read, Reason & REFLECT!

# DR. PARMENTER'S
# MAGNETIC OIL!
## Will Cure Rheumatism!

## TO THOSE AFFLICTED!

This Oil is warranted to ease more pain in less time, than any other medicine now in use. Call and test its Virtue; it removes the worst Rheumatic pain in 30 minutes; pains in the side, breast and back, in 20 minutes; Nervous Headache in 10 minutes; Croup in 20 minutes; Chilblains in one night, and is a sure cure for chapped hands. The Oil acts on the System on the principle of Electricity, regulates the whole system, and is perfectly safe in all cases. **PRICE 25 CENTS PER BOTTLE.**

# PRINCIPAL DEPOT,
## No. 9 Cooper's Buildings, cor. State & Green Sts.,
ALBANY, N. Y., and for sale by Druggists generally, throughout the United States and the Canadas. Druggists, Merchants and Peddlers supplied at the lowest prices,

## By Dr. WM. O. PARMENTER.

BAKER TAYLOR, PRINTER, 58 STATE STREET, ALBANY.

# MERCHANT'S GARGLING OIL

(FIRST INTRODUCED 1833)

## A Liniment For Man And Beast

### Yellow Wrapper for Animal and White for Human Flesh.

**THE BEST EMBROCATION OF THE WORLD FOR**

CATTLE • HORSES • POULTRY • FANCY STOCK

Medium Size.    Large Size.    Small Size.    Small Size.

FOR ANIMAL USE PRICE 50 CTS.    FOR ANIMAL USE PRICE $1.00    FOR FAMILY USE PRICE 25 CTS    FOR ANIMAL USE PRICE 25 CTS.

Manufactured by **MERCHANT'S GARGLING OIL COMPANY.**
LOCKPORT. N.Y., U.S.A.

© PORTAL PUBLICATIONS, SAUSALITO, CALIF. 94965

72. Chromolithograph poster, New York, 1862–68. *New-York Historical Society, Bella C. Landauer Collection.*

◁ 71. Chromolithograph trade card, Sausalito, California, 1894. *Woodrow Gelman Collection.*

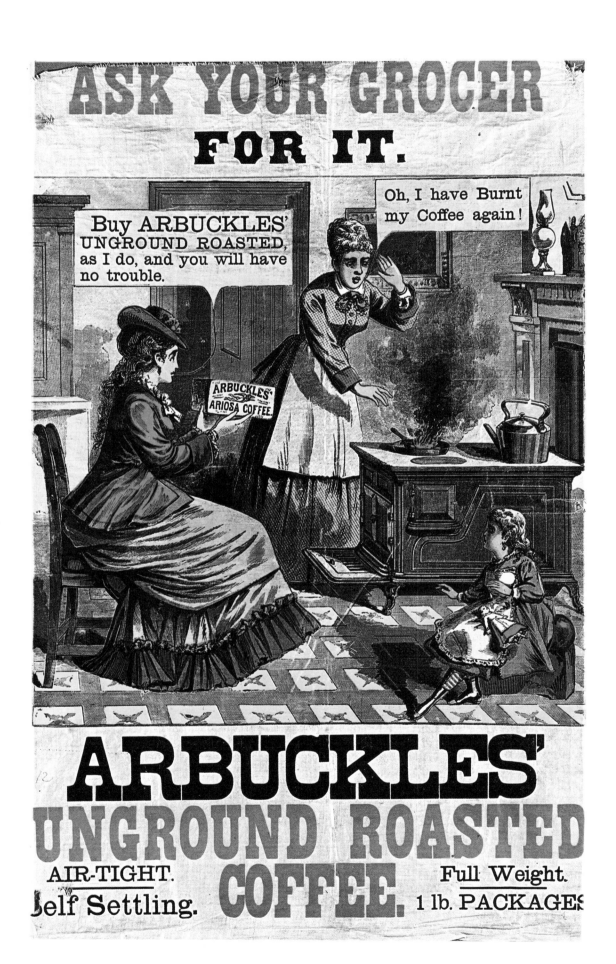

73. Chromolithograph poster, 1880s. *New-York Historical Society, Bella C. Landauer Collection.*

74. Chromolithograph poster, New York, 1862–68. *New-York Historical Society, Bella C. Landauer Collection.* ▷

# USE

## THE ILLINOIS STARCH CO'S

# OSCEOLA STARCH

LITH. IN COLORS BY CHAS HART, 99 FULTON ST. N.Y.

# JOSIAH MACY'S SONS AGT.
## NEW YORK.

75. Chromolithograph poster, New York, 1870s. *New-York Historical Society.*

76. Chromolithograph poster, Sausalito, California, 1890. *Woodrow Gelman Collection.* ▷

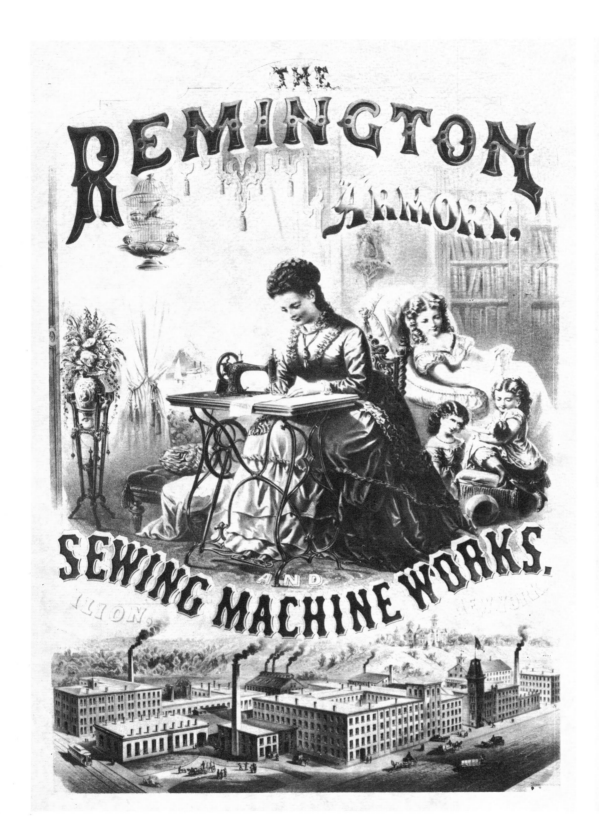

77. Chromolithograph poster, 1870s. *New-York Historical Society, Bella C. Landauer Collection.*

78 a and b. Patent medicine advertisement. Lithograph. *New-York Historical Society, Bella C. Landauer Collection.*

79. Cigarette insert cards. *New York, Metropolitan Museum of Art, Burdick Collection.* ▷

80 and 81. Chromolithograph trade cards for chocolate, 1880s. *New-York Historical Society.* ▷

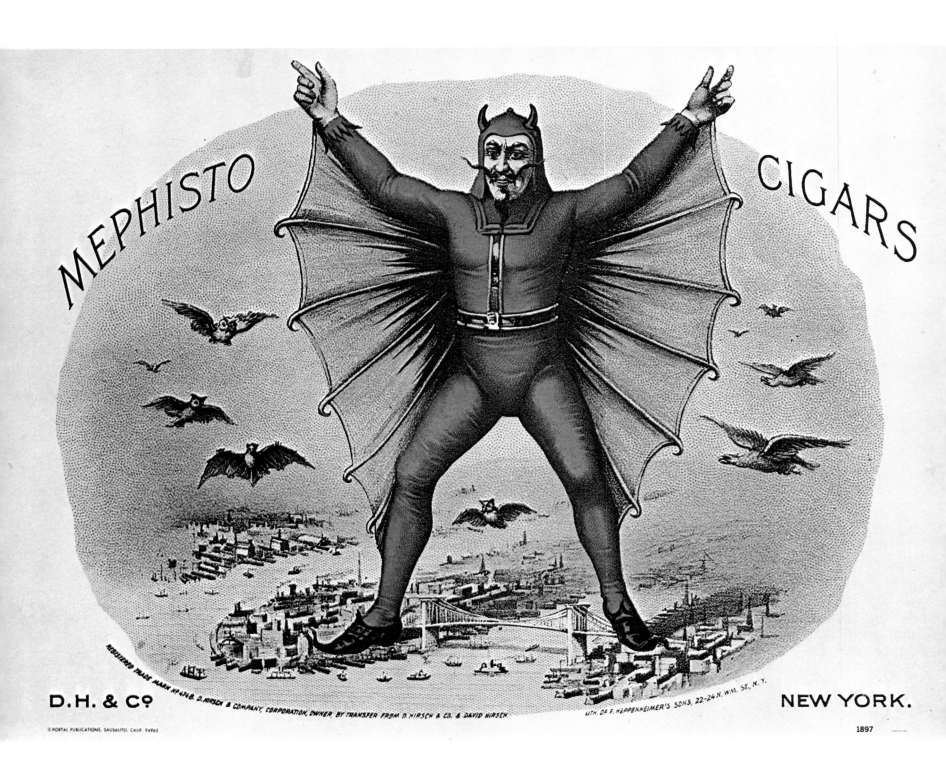

82. Chromolithograph cigar box label, Sausalito, California, 1897. *Woodrow Gelman Collection.*

83. Chromolithograph poster, 1880s.
*New-York Historical Society, Bella C. Landauer Collection.*

84 and 85. Chromolithograph trade cards, 1880s. *New-York Historical Society.*

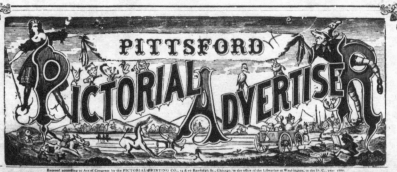

86. Wood-engraved advertisement, Vermont, 1882.
*New-York Historical Society, Bella C. Landauer Collection.*

87. Wood-engraved advertisement, Vermont, 1880s.
*New-York Historical Society, Bella C. Landauer Collection.*

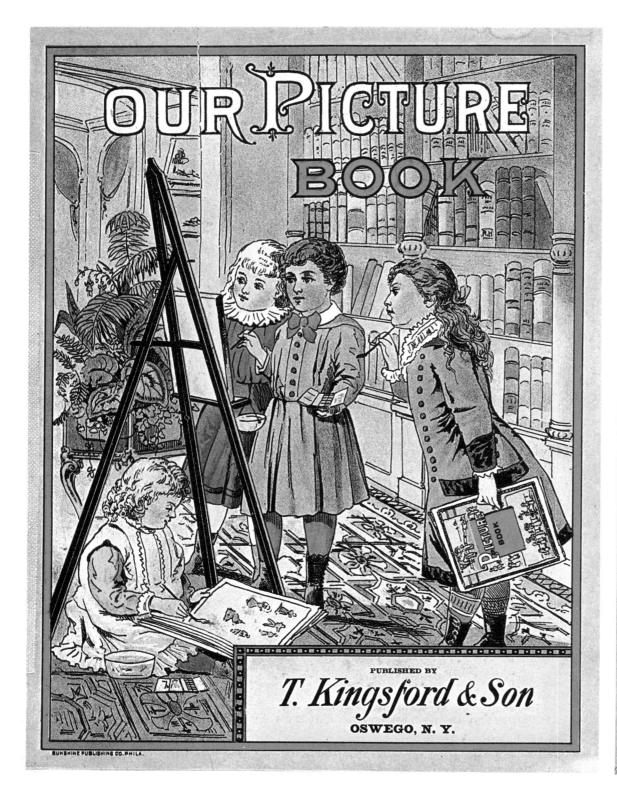

88. Chromolithograph poster, Philadelphia, about 1900. *New-York Historical Society, Bella C. Landauer Collection.*

89. Chromolithograph poster, New York, 1927. *New-York Historical Society, Bella C. Landauer Collection.*

90. Chromolithograph poster, about 1900. *New-York Historical Society, Bella C. Landauer Collection.*

91. Chromolithograph poster, Boston, about 1900. *New-York Historical Society, Bella C. Landauer Collection.* ▷

To the Honourable
RIP VAN DAM, Esqr
PRESIDENT of His Majestys Council for the PROVINCE of NEW YORK
This View of the New Dutch Church is most humbly
Dedicated by your Honours most Obedient Servt Wm Burgis

92. The Dutch Reformed Church, built 1727-31 on the corner of Nassau and Liberty streets, New York.
On the right, the Eglise du Saint-Esprit, built in 1704.
The coach is Rip Van Dam's. *New York, Metropolitan Museum of Art, gift of William Loring Andrews.*

93. Chromolithograph poster, 1888. *New-York Historical Society, Bella C. Landauer Collection.* ▷

A WRITING DESK FOR EVERY HOME

THE "ECONOMY" WALL DESK
CORTLAND DESK CO. LIMITED.
CORTLAND, N.Y.

PATENTED FEB 8 1887.          COPYRIGHT 1888

New England Agent, GEO. S. DELANO, New Medford, Mass.

DISTRIBUTING SHIP CARGO OF STANDARD BUGGIES COAST OF AUSTRALIA

94. Chromolithograph poster, about 1880. *New-York Historical Society, Bella C. Landauer Collection.*

95. Chromolitograph poster, Boston, 1890s. *New-York Historical Society, Bella C. Landauer Collection.* ▷

96. Stage Coach passing the Astor House Hotel, New York 1845. Lithograph. *New-York Historical Society.*

97. Lithographic music cover, New York, 1896. *New-York Historical Society.*

98. Charter of the coach makers' union. Lithograph, Philadelphia, 1840s. *New-York Historical Society.* ▷

99. Chromolithograph poster, New York, 1890s. *New York, Metropolitan Museum of Art, gift of Bessie Potter Vonnoh.*

100. Sheet music cover, New York, about 1910. *Woodrow Gelman Collection.*

101. Process color illustration by R. Fouteault in "The World," August, 1896. *Woodrow Gelman Collection.* ▷

# The True Story of Mr. Blue Beard.

Many years ago there lived a nobleman who possessed some wealth, but not enough to be the high-flyer his ancestors had been, nor yet enough to

"Come on and be killed, Madam!" roared Blue Beard from the bottom of the stairs a minute later.

enew the plumbing and make other re-airs in his ancestral castles.

Therefore he hied himself off to merica in search of an American eiress who would jump at the chance f exchanging her fortune for a title d a fixed residence in dear old England. He had heard that our grand ee country had in it a number of feeble-inded females of this kind, and when arrived on our shores he found that e report was quite true, and that he uld have his pick and choice of a rge number of American heiresses, re-ardless of the fact that he was a tzened, shrunken, evil-looking old retch, with so little moral character t that it would have taken the big lescope at the Lick observatory to ave discovered it. He was a choice ecimen of the type of individuals we ll "a tough." He had, moreover, an digo blue beard, but his title would ve made him eligible to a certain pe of the American heiress had he en ringed, streaked and striped with pea-green beard.

Blue Beard, after being lionized to en his own disgust at Newport, Bar arbor and Lenox, and after rejecting e offers of many heiresses, decided on one of two sisters as the future rs. Blue Beard. Her name was Fatima. t as she was a young lady of the st generous physical proportions she s playfully called Fatty by her inti-ates. Her sister's name was Anne. ey were shrewd young women in me respects, and they wished to be ad sure that Blue Beard's castle was t a fake. Expressing this wish to him invited them to go over to England d see it for themselves. The young dies accepted the invitation and were on in England, where they satisfied emselves that the castle and the bleman's social standing were all he ha... presented, whereupon Fatty threw herself into his arms, saying:

"My noble, generous lord! I am yours, for I am sure, quite sure, that I love you now."

"My own darling!" he said, embracing as much of her as he could reach around, "I have you not only on your own account, but on your bank account."

"It is all yours," she murmured.

Fatty and Anne then returned to New York, and the wedding, which came off in Grace Church, is talked about to this day. All of the Four Hundred were there, and at the close of the ceremony they fairly climbed over each other's heads and tore each other's clothes in their frantic endeavors to possess themselves of the flowers Blue Beard had imported for the occasion from his English conservatories. The strife for these souvenirs of nobility was so hot and eager that the famous Mrs. Van Million, who was noted for her regal manners, came out of the church with her magnificent Worth gown in rags and her $100 Virot bonnet torn from her head, while her beautiful wavy false front dangled over one ear.

The haughty Mrs. K. De Forest De Ducats so far forgot herself as to accuse the superb Mrs. Royal St. Hauteur of being "no lady" because that individual snatched a choice rose that Blue Beard's own royal foot had trod upon from Mrs. De Ducat's hand after she had crawled under ten pews of the church to get possession of this souvenir of royalty. The police had to come in and use their clubs to restore order, and it was extremely mortifying to the proud family of Fatty to have her carefully planned and enormously expensive English wedding partake so largely of the elements of an Irish wake.

Fatty's gown was a Worth creation of ivory-white satin, with a train so long and so profuse in real old point lace that it filled many a woman with such envy that she would willingly have torn it to rags rather than to have had Fatty possess it. She wore an enormous diamond sunburst and a diamnd necklace and tiara, gifts of the generous Blue Beard, the bills for which were sent to Fatty's father. This was all very lovely for Fatty, and it put Blue Beard into such a good humor that he was kind and polite to his wife for nearly a week after the wedding.

They sailed for England amid the loudly uttered good wishes of many who at heart wished that the Cunarder Blue Beard and his wife were on would go to the bottom of the ocean rather than that Fatty should reap the rewards of what she had paid the money for.

Two days after their arrival at Blue Beard's castle he said to Fatty:

"My dear Fat, I must go away to see a man and may be gone a day or two. Here are the keys of the castle. You may go all over it and may enter every room but the blue chamber. Keep out of that, or you'll wish you had. I do not desire to be harsh to my dear Fatty, but if you go into that room there'll be a regular monkey and parrot time of it when I get home. You hear me?"

"Yes, my lord," replied Fatty. But the moment Blue Beard was gone Fatty ran to her sister, who was visiting her, and said:

"What do you think, Anne? My lord says I am not to enter the blue chamber while he is away."

"I guess I'd show him that I'd enter any room I pleased in this house after all the money you've got to spend on it to put it into decent shape," said Anne, with much asperity.

"I'd just like to know what's in that room," said Fatty.

"Why don't you go and see?"

"He might not like it."

"Pooh! Now see here, Fatty; if you give in to your husband in the beginning you'll have it to do all of the time. I'd just let him know at the outset that I came from a country in which a wife is not only the equal, but a good deal the superior of her husband. I'd like to see the man who could boss me!"

"I dare say that you would," said Fatima, a little tartly, "but I believe that you are right, so come on and we'll see what's in that room, and if Blue Beard don't like it he can lump it."

So the two sisters went to the blue chamber and Fatty opened the door and stepped in.

"My soul and body!" she exclaimed, throwing up both hands and dropping the key, whereupon it fell with a dull thud to the floor, and Fatima came near following suit, for there, ranged along the wall, were the thirteen dead wives of Blue Beard, while above each hung a life-size Rembrandt of herself.

"The old wretch, to go and make a cemetery of his own house!" said Anne. "He's a regular Holmes! If I were you, he'd hear from me the moment he got home, and there'd be some house-cleaning done here and those ladies should be carted off to the crematory."

"It's where they belong," said Fatima. "I call it anything but pleasant to have them around here. But what is that? Oh, Anne, it is Blue Beard returning already!" She picked up the key and found that there was a drop of blood on it she could not wash off. While she was rubbing away at it Blue Beard came in and, striking an attitude, said:

"Aha, madam! What do I see? My orders have been disobeyed. Your life shall pay the penalty of this wilful disobedience!"

"Now, don't get rattled," said Fatima, calmly seeking to engage her lord in a dispute while Anne went down to the telephone and rang up No. 642, which was the police station.

"Madam!" roared Blue Beard, "your time is short!"

"Spare me long enough to crimp my bangs," said Fatima with true American spirit and independence, feeling buoyantly confident that America had beaten England once and could do it again.

Blue Beard was dazed by this splendid exhibition of nerve. He could not but admire Fatima's courage, and he said:

"Well, you're a good one. Time to crimp of your hair? Well, I like that! I'll give you ten minutes while I go down to the grindstone and sharpen my sword."

"Thanks!" said Fatima, tittering in her sleeve. Then she joined Anne, and said:

"Did you ring up the police station?"

"Yes, and the patrol wagon is now on its way to the house."

"Good enough," said the plucky Fatima; "it'll just about paralyze my precious husband when he sees it."

Come on and be killed, Madam!" roared Blue Beard from the bottom of the stairs a few minutes later.

"Coming, dear," replied Fatima, airily, for she had caught sight of four of the "finest" coming towards her house. When Blue Beard saw them enter the door he hissed out:

"Betrayed! But I'll never be taken alive!" Nor was he. When they dragged him from his hiding place a few minutes later it was found that he had swallowed an enormous dose of Rough on Rats, and in three minutes Fatima was a widow.

"And the social season at its height," said Fatima, sadly. "But black is wonderfully becoming to me," she added more cheerfully.

Fatima's first care was to have her thirteen predecessors cremated along with the husband who had been so much to them in life, and when her year of mourning was done she became one of the most dashing widows England had ever known.

MAX MERRYMAN.

# "Sezi" and "Sezee."

She was a "saleslady" of the type that chews gum and wears fourteen rings on one hand, the aggregate value of the lot being about a dollar and seventy-five cents. She had had a "falling-out" with her "best fellow" and was giving an account of the tragic event to another "saleslady," whose own wad of tutti-frutti was gracefully poised between her half-parted lips.

"Yes, Mag," said the bejewelled saleslady, "I've give him the G. B. for good and all."

"La, Mame, you ain't!"

"Ain't I, though? Well, I guess. I let him know that I don't play second fiddle to no fellow an' that he couldn't take Jennie Simpson to the ice-cream saloon one night and take me to walk round in the park next night an' never get me so much as a soda. I guess I paralyzed him!"

"What did he say?"

"Well, I'll tell you the whole story, Mag. I didn't let out on 'im till we'd got clean back to our house and then sezi to him, sezi:

"'You think you're blamed smart, don't you, Jim Hixon,' sezi, an' he sez, sezee:

"'What do you mean, Mame?' sezee, an' sezi to him, sezi:

"'Oh, you're mighty innocent, now, ain't you?' sezi, an' he sez, sezee:

"'Pon honor, Mame, I don't know what you're drivin' at,' an' I up an' sez, sezi:

"'You don't know anything about a certain feller takin' a certain freckle-nosed, tallow-complexioned, pop-eyed, lop-eared girl to the ice-cream saloon last night, now, do you?' sezi, right out, flat-footed, like that, an' he looked as if he'd drop, an' he sez, sezee:

"'So you're onto that, are you, Mame,' an' I sez, sezi:

"'Yes, I am, my youthful friend, an' I'm onto the rest of your curves,' sezi, 'an' I'll thank you to address me as Miss Hobbs hereafter,' sezi, 'an' I don't want you to even speak to me on the street,' sezi, 'for you're no more to me than the dirt an' grime under my feet,' sezi, 'an' if you think, Jim Hixon, that I'll play second fiddle to Jen Simpson you're most beautifully left,' sezi. 'I'm accustomed to receiving attentions from gentlemen, an' I'm sorry I ever lowered myself by condescending to even look at such a squint-eyed, bow-legged, pimple-faced, drab-haired chump as you are,' sezi."

"Oh, Mame, you didn't?"

"Didn't I though? I tell you my dander was up an' I let 'im have it right in the neck."

"'The next time a lady condescends to look at you,' sezi, 'an' give you her comp'ny, I hope you'll treat her as a lady expects to be treated,' sezi, an' he sez, sezee:

"'Shucks, Mame!' sezee; 'you know I don't care two wrappings of my finger for Jen,' sezee, an' I sez, sezi:

"'That's more'n I care for you, Jim Hixon, an' now you git,' sezi."

"La, Mame, what did he do?"

"He got."

"He did?"

"You kin just bet he did."

"An' ain't you goin' to make it up with 'im?"

"Me? What you take me for, Mag Higgins? When I go to craw fishin' you'll know it, for—there's the floor-walker watchin' us, the old bloke."

# The "All Right" Friend.

I'm not well posted in the tricks
Of policy or politics;
The East and West can fight it out—
I don't know what it's all about.
But I am waiting till the time
Allows me to commit a crime.
I wish to single out the man,
And slaughter him, that's if I can—
The man who on election night
Insists on saying "He's all right!"

LA TOUCHE HANCOCK.

## FRANKNESS.

She—To what am I indebted for the pleasure of this call?

He—To the fact that the other girl I called on was not at home.

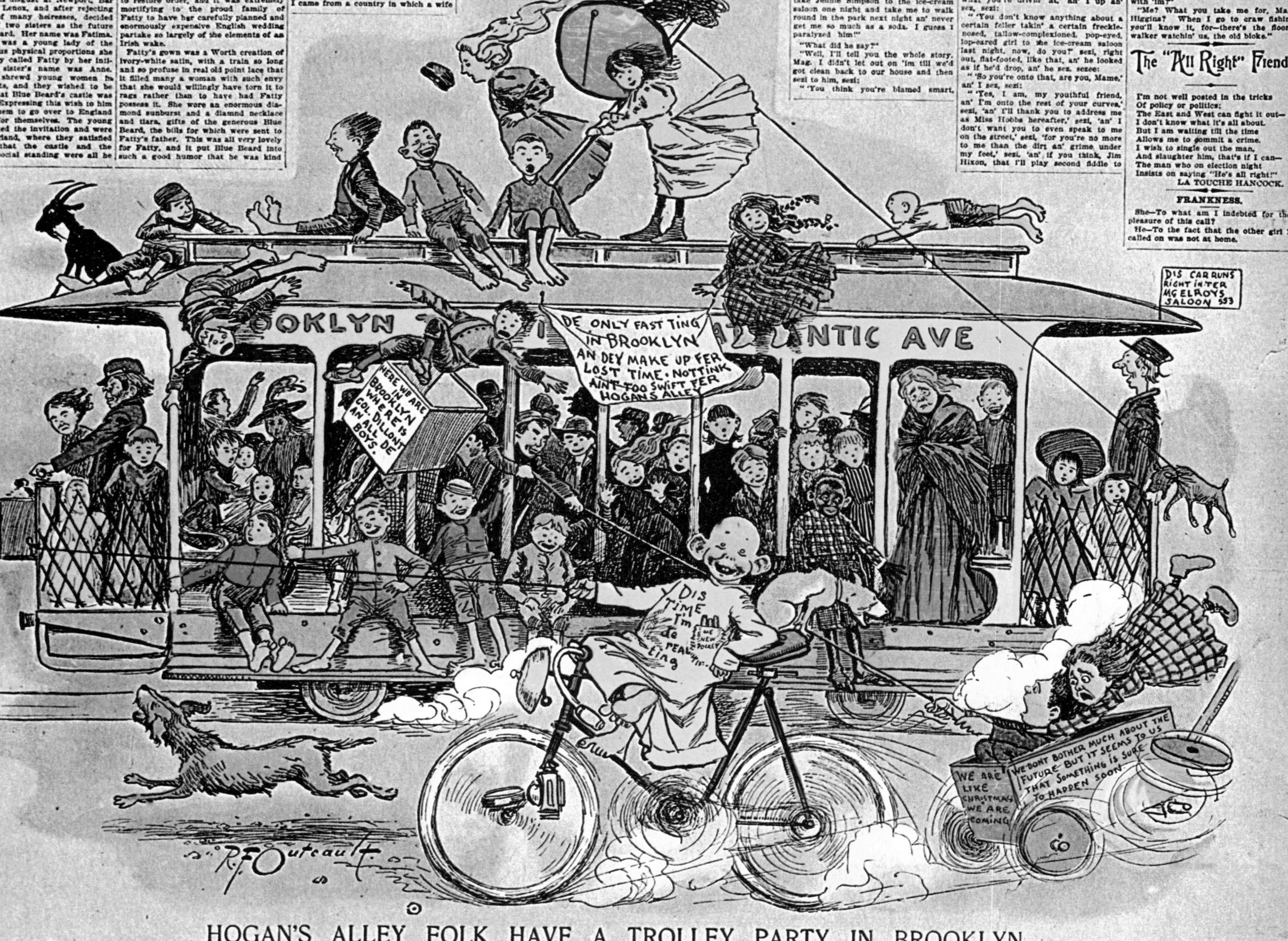


HOGAN'S ALLEY FOLK HAVE A TROLLEY PARTY IN BROOKLYN.

# PRINCE'S, AERIAL SHIP. STAR OF THE EAST!

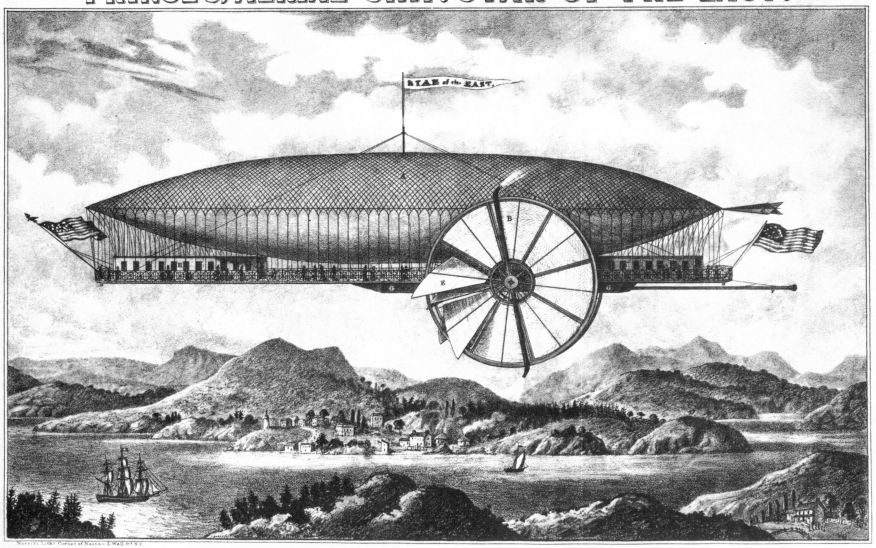

REFERENCE.

A. Balloon or Envelope composed of Gum Elastic length 300 feet Diam 50 ft. _ B. Propelling wheel whose Fans are open at 60 and 80 degrees with the Horizon. _ C. Agitating Vane or Rudder. _ D.D. Car composed of Willow. H.H. Cabins of Willow. _ E. Fan open _ G.G. Receiver for rarefying the Air. _ F. Draft pipe.

102. Lithograph, New York, 1830s.
*New York, Metropolitan Museum of Art, gift of Paul Bird, Jr.*

103. Clipper *Dreadnaught* 12½ days from New York on her celebrated passage into dock at Liverpool in 12 days, 11 hours, December 1854. *New York, Metropolitan Museum of Art, A. S. Colgate gift.*

U. S. FRIGATE CONSTITUTION, of 44 GUNS.

104. The *Constitution*, built in Philadelphia, 1797. Fought the *Guerrière* and the *Java* in the War of 1812. Aquatint by Abel Bowen. *New York, Metropolitan Museum of Art.*

PUBLISHED BY N. CURRIER 152 NASSAU ST NEW YORK

## THE CLIPPER YACHT "AMERICA".

**DIMENSIONS:**

TONNAGE — 170
LENGTH OF KEEL — 62 FT
LENGTH ON DECK — 94
EXTREME BREADTH — 22½
BREADTH MOULDED — 22
DEPTH OF HOLD — 9 FT½

WINNER OF THE ROYAL YACHT SQUADRON CUP VALUE £100...IN THE GREAT MATCH FOR ALL NATIONS AT COWES AUGUST 22ND AND OF A MATCH WITH THE TITANIA FOR £100. AUGUST 28TH 1851.

Built by Mr George Steers of New York for Jno C Stevens Esqr and associates of the New York Yacht Club

**SPARS:**

FORE MAST — 79 FT. 6 INCH
MAIN MAST — 81
BOW SPRIT (HOLLOW) 32 — 17 FT. OUT BOARD.
FORE GAFF — 24
MAIN — 28
MAIN BOOM — 58

2½ INCH TO FOOT RAKE.

105. Yacht *America* after winning the Cowes race, 1851. Hand-colored lithograph by Currier & Ives.
New York, *Metropolitan Museum of Art, A. S. Colgate gift.*

CLIPPER SHIP "COMET" OF NEW YORK.

IN A HURRICANE OFF BERMUDA, ON HER VOYAGE FROM NEW YORK TO SAN FRANCISCO, OCT? 1852.

NEW YORK, PUBLISHED BY N. CURRIER, 152 NASSAU STREET.

106. Clipper *Comet* on her record voyage, 103 days from New York to San Francisco, 1852.
*New York, Metropolitan Museum of Art, A. S. Colgate gift.*

Merchants' Express Line of Clipper Ships
F R
# SAN FRANCISCO!

NONE BUT A 1 FAST SAILING CLIPPERS LOADED IN THIS LINE.

### THE EXTREME CLIPPER SHIP

# OCEAN EXPRESS

WATSON, COMMANDER,

## AT PIER 9, EAST RIVER.

This splendid vessel is one of the fastest Clippers afloat, and a great favorite with all shippers. Her commander, Capt. WATSON, was formerly master of the celebrated Clipper "FLYING DRAGON," which made the passage in **97 days,** and of the ship POLYNESIA, which made the passage in **103 days.**

She comes to the berth one third loaded, and has very large engagements.

## RANDOLPH M. COOLEY,

118 WATER ST., cor. Wall, Tontine Building.

Agents in San Francisco, DE WITT, KITTLE & Co.

NESBITT & CO., PRINTERS.

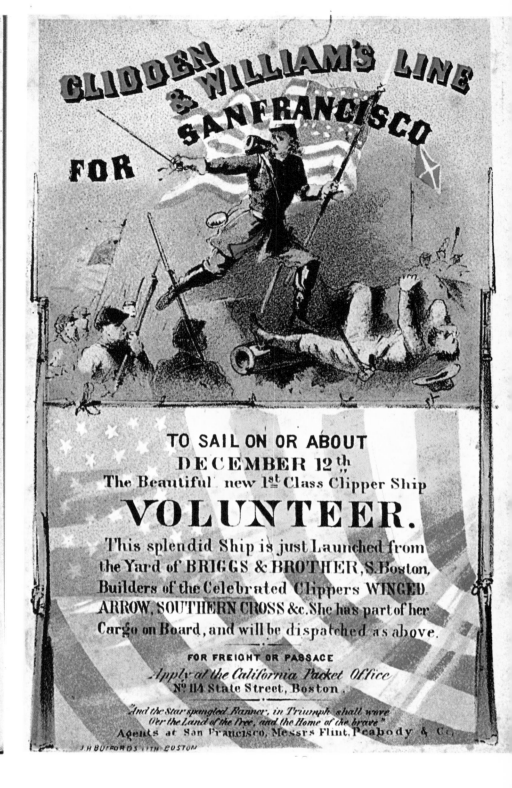

GLIDDEN & WILLIAM'S LINE
FOR SAN FRANCISCO

TO SAIL ON OR ABOUT
DECEMBER 12th
The Beautiful new 1st Class Clipper Ship

# VOLUNTEER.

This splendid Ship is just Launched from the Yard of BRIGGS & BROTHER, S. Boston, Builders of the Celebrated Clippers WINGED ARROW, SOUTHERN CROSS &c. She has part of her Cargo on Board, and will be dispatched as above.

FOR FREIGHT OR PASSAGE

*Apply at the California Packet Office*
Nº 114 State Street, Boston.

*"And the Star spangled Banner, in Triumph shall wave*
*Oer the Land of the Free, and the Home of the brave"*
Agents at San Francisco, Messrs Flint, Peabody & Co

J.H.BUFFORDS LITH BOSTON

107. Clipper ship card. Chromolithograph, New York, 1850s.
*Woodrow Gelman Collection.*

108. Clipper ship card. Chromolithograph, Boston, 1850s.
*Woodrow Gelman Collection.*

109. Ladies' Saloon on a Hudson River Steamboat. Lithograph, New York, about 1840. *New-York Historical Society, Bella C. Landauer Collection.*

110. British twin-screw steamboat in Philadelphia, 1839. *Historical Society of Pennsylvania.*

111. Hudson river steamboat. Relief wood or metal engraving, Albany, 1810-13. *New-York Historical Society.* ▷

# WRITING BOOK.

THE PROPERTY OF

*Miss nSatra Remington*

—— 1813 ——

Bought of Websters and Skinners, at their
Bookstore, corner of State & Pearl-streets,
Albany.

# Writing and Cyphering Books,

Wholesale and Retail, and a general supply of Classical, School and other Books, and Station-
ary, constantly for sale at Websters and Skinners' Bookstore, Albany.

*ALSO,*

The Easy Instructor, or New Method of Teaching Sacred Music.

"ROUNDING A BEND" ON THE MISSISSIPPI.

The parting Salute

NEW YORK, PUBLISHED BY CURRIER & IVES, 152 NASSAU ST.

112. Racing steamboats. Hand-colored lithograph after Frances F. Palmer, by Currier & Ives, New York, 1866.
*New York, Metropolitan Museum of Art, A. S. Colgate gift.*

Awful Conflagration of the Steam Boat **LEXINGTON** In Long Island Sound on Monday Eve.ᵍ Janᵞ 13ᵗʰ 1840. by which melancholy occurrence, over 100 PERSONS PERISHED.

113. The burning of the *Lexington* in Long Island Sound. Hand colored lithograph by Nathaniel Currier, New York, 1840. *New York, Metropolitan Museum of Art, A. S. Colgate gift.*

CONFLAGRATION of the STEAM BOAT NEW JERSEY on the DELAWARE RIVER opposite PHILADA.
March 15th 1856, in which 60 Persons lost their Lives

RAILROAD DEPOT AT PHILADELPHIA.

114. Lithograph, Philadelphia, 1856. *New York Public Library*.

115. Philadelphia's first Railway station. Lithograph, 1832. *Historical Society of Pennsylvania*.

A. MAJOR, Publisher, 330 Pearl St., N.Y.

| JOHN A. ROEBLING, C. E. | DESIGNER OF BRIDGE | NEW YORK TOWER | **BIRD'S-EYE VIEW OF THE GREAT NEW YORK AND BROOKLYN BRIDGE,** | BROOKLYN TOWER | WILLIAM VANDERBOSCH. | |
| WASHINGTON A. ROEBLING, | CHIEF ENGINEER | | | | WILLIAM HILDENBRAND. | DRAUGHTSMEN |
| CHARLES C. MARTIN, | 1ST ASST. ENGINEER | | AND GRAND DISPLAY OF FIRE WORKS ON OPENING NIGHT. | | E. F. FARRINGTON. | |
| FRANCIS COLLINGWOOD, | | | | | THOS. G. DOUGLAS. | MASTER MECHANIC |
| COL. WM. H. PAINE, | ENGINEERS. | | | | CHAS. W. YOUNG | SUPT. OF MASONRY |
| GEO. W. McNULTY. | | | | | | GENL. FOREMAN OF LABORERS. |

[ PYROTECHNICS FURNISHED BY DETWILLER & STREET, NEW YORK. ]

COMMENCED JANUARY 3, 1870.                    FINISHED MAY 24, 1883.

The Bridge crosses the river by a single span of 1596 ft., suspended by four cables 15¾ ins. in diameter; each cable consists of 5,434 parallel steel wires; ultimate strength of each cable 11,200 tons.   The approach on the New York side is 1,492½ ft., approach on the Brooklyn side 1,901 ft., total length 5,989 ft.   Size of towers at high water line 140x59 ft., total height of Towers 277 ft.   From high water to roadway 120 ft.,—from high water to centre of span 138 ft.,—from roadway to top 158 ft.,—width of Bridge 85 ft., with tracks for steam cars, roadway for carriages, and walks for foot passengers, and an elevated promenade commanding a view of extraordinary beauty and extent.   Cost, $15,000,000.

116. The opening of Brooklyn Bridge, May, 1883. Lithograph by A. Major, New York. *New York, Metropolitan Museum of Art, Edwin C. Arnold gift.*

117. Chromolithograph poster, 1880s. *New-York Historical Society, Bella C. Landauer Collection.*

118. Town truss bridge for the Philadelphia, Germantown & Norristown Railway. Lithograph, 1834. *Historical Society of Pennsylvania.*

119. Wood-engraved poster, Elmira, New York, 1853. *New-York Historical Society, Bella C. Landauer Collection.* ▷

# FRESH OYSTERS!

## BY WESTOVERS' AMBOY LINE.

### Through by Express on the
## NEW YORK & ERIE RAIL ROAD.

### For Sale Here,

**And by the Proprietors, in all the Principal** Towns on the New York & Erie Railroad, and also on the *Chenango Valley*, from *Binghamton* to *Utica*.

**Customers dealing with this Line shall be sup-**plied regularly, according to order, through the season, with the best of AMBOY OYSTERS, at the lowest possible prices.

*Sept.* 10, 1853.          **C. & R. WESTOVER.**

[From Fairmans' Job Printing Office, Elmira.]

AMERICAN RAILROAD SCENE.

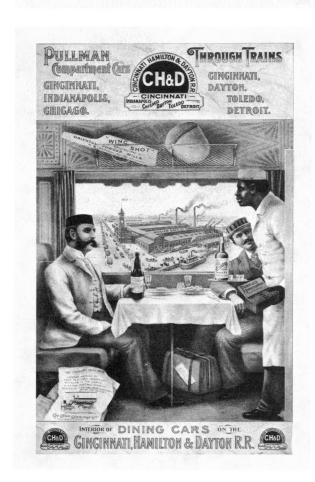

120. Hand-colored lithograph, Currier & Ives, New York, 1871. *New York, Metropolitan Museum of Art, A. S. Colgate gift.*

121. Chromolithograph poster, Cincinnati, 1890s. *New-York Historical Society, Bella C. Landauer Collection.*

122. Chromolithograph poster, about 1890. *New-York Historical Society, Bella C. Landauer Collection.*

123. Chromolithograph poster, 1897. *New-York Historical Society, Bella C. Landauer Collection.* ▷

WORCESTER SALT SPECIAL,
162 Cars started by President-Elect, William McKinley.
TRAIN NEARLY ONE AND A HALF MILES LONG.
OVER 5,000,000 lbs WORCESTER SALT PACKED IN 725,613 BAGS, 50,000 CARTONS, 7,000 LARGE SACKS
ENOUGH TO SEASON 100,000,000 lbs. OF BUTTER.

THE BARRELS PILED END ON END          THE BAGS LAID IN A ROW
WOULD BE OVER SIX MILES HIGH.          WOULD EXTEND 131 MILES.
THE LARGEST SINGLE SHIPMENT OF A MANUFACTURED COMMODITY EVER MADE.

TRAIN SHIPPED FROM
WORCESTER SALT FACTORY, SILVER SPRINGS, N.Y.
JAN. 6TH 1897 VIA ERIE. AND N.Y. N.H & H.R.R.
TO NEW ENGLAND POINTS.

124. Chromolithograph by Currier & Ives, 1884. *New York, Metropolitan Museum of Art, gift of A. S. Colgate.*

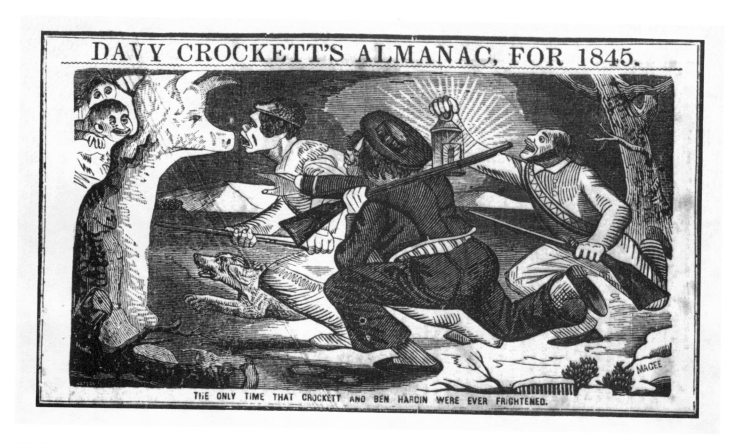

THE ONLY TIME THAT CROCKETT AND BEN HARDIN WERE EVER FRIGHTENED.

Old Block's Cabin.—See page 1.

125. Wood engraving in *Davy Crockett's Almanac*, New York, 1845.
*New York, Metropolitan Museum of Art.*

126. Alonzo Delano: *Old Block's Sketch-Book; or, Tales of California Life*, Sacramento, 1856.
*Princeton University Library, gift of Sinclair Hamilton.*

THE MINING BUSINESS IN FOUR PICTURES.

GOING IN TO IT.     MAKING SOMETHING.

MAKING NOTHING.     GOING OUT OF IT.

127. Lithograph letter paper by Joseph Britton, San Francisco, 1850s. *New-York Historical Society.*

128. Lithograph letter paper, Britton & Rey, San Francisco, 1850s. *New-York Historical Society.*

129. Pictorial letter paper. Lithograph by Britton and Rey, San Francisco, 1850s. *New-York Historical Society.* ▷

MINERS WEIGHING THEIR GOLD.

**THE DREAM OF A PROSPECTING MINER.**
Lith. & Published by Britton & Rey corner Montgomery & California Sts S. Francisco.

TREMENDOUS EXCITEMENT !

Samuel Whittaker and Robert McKenzie rescued from the authorities, and hung by the Vigilance Committee, on Sunday August 24th at 3 o'clock P.M. in the presence of Fifteen thousand People.

POST OFFICE, SAN FRANCISCO, CALIFORNIA.

130. Vigilante executions, San Francisco, August, 1851. Lithograph. *New-York Historical Society.*

131. San Francisco Post Office, opened 1854. Lithograph by William Endicott. *New-York Historical Society.*

132. Lithograph letter paper, Britton & Rey, San Francisco, 1850s. *New-York Historical Society.* ▷

Bar Room in the Mines

Long Tom.

Lith & Published by Britton & Rey S. Fs

# SARONI, ARCHER & Cº

### CLAY STREET, BETWEEN MONTGOMERY & KEARNY STS, SAN-FRANCISCO, CALIFORNIA.

Hat, Cap & Gents Furnishing Store, have constantly on hand, and continually import the latest Style of every description of Gents Hats, Ladies Riding Hats, Whips and Gloves, Youths and Childrens Hats & Caps, and a large assortment of Gentlemens Furnishing Goods, Umbrellas, Canes, Hair Brushes, Portmoneys, and Gents Dressing Cases.

### WHOLESALE & RETAIL.
Hats & Caps made to order.

LITH. DE SARONY & MAJOR 117 FULTON ST. N YORK

LIFE IN THE COUNTRY

THE RETURN FROM THE PASTURE

134. Life in the country. Hand-colored lithograph by Currier & Ives after Frances Bond Palmer, 1862. *New York, Metropolitan Museum of Art, A.S. Colgate gift.*

135. The return from the pasture. Hand-colored lithograph by Currier & Ives after Frances Bond Palmer. *New York, Metropolitan Museum of Art, A.S. Colgate gift.*

◁ 133. Poster for Saroni, Archer clothing store, San Francisco. Lithograph by Sarony & Major, New York, 1850s. *New-York Historical Society.*

136. The burning of the Crystal Palace, New York, 1858. Hand-colored lithograph by Currier & Ives. *New-York Historical Society.*

BIRDS EYE VIEW
OF
GREENWOOD CEMETERY.

137. Greenwood Cemetery, Brooklyn. Lithograph by J. Bachmann, New York. *New York, Metropolitan Museum of Art*.

138. The oyster man. Lithograph by August Köllner in *Common Sights in Town and Country*, Philadelphia, about 1850.
*New York, Metropolitan Museum of Art, Dick Fund.*

139. Chromolithograph poster, Ilion, N. Y., 1890s. *New-York Historical Society, Bella C. Landauer Collection.*

140. The burning of the Crystal Palace, New York, October 5th, 1858. Lithograph. *New-York Historical Society.*

141. Lithograph music cover, probably copied from a daguerreotype, New York, 1849. *New-York Historical Society.* ▷

# DILIGENT HOSE COMP.

## QUICK STEP.

As performed by

# DODWORTH'S

*Cornet Band of New York.*


Price 25 cts Nett.

NEW-YORK,
PUBLISHED BY Wm. HALL & SON, 239 BROADWAY, (OPPOSITE THE PARK.)
EDWd. WALKER, 160, CHESNUT St. PHILa.

Entered according to act of Congress in the Year 1849, by Wm. Hall & Son, in the Clerk's Office of the Dist. Court of the South. Dist. of N.Y.

SHAKERS near LEBANON, their mode of WORSHIP.

142. Shakers dancing to shake the evil out of their bodies. Lithograph, 1830s. *New-York Historical Society.*

METHODIST CAMP MEETING.

143. Camp meeting, 1837. Lithograph by E. W. Clay. *New-York Historical Society.*

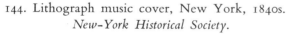

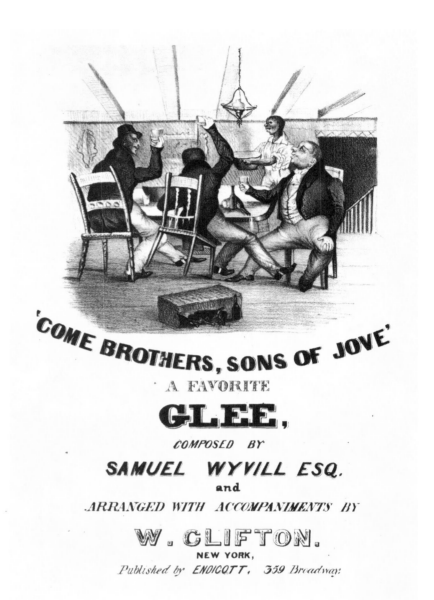

144. Lithograph music cover, New York, 1840s.
*New-York Historical Society.*

145. Lithograph music cover, New York, 1834-36.
*New-York Historical Society.*

146. Lithograph music cover, Boston, 1840. *New-York Historical Society.* ▷

# The Pirate's Glee.

WORDS BY

### ARTHUR MORRILL ESQ.

*Music Composed & Respectfully dedicated to the*

## SALEM GLEE CLUB.

BY

### BENJAMIN F. BAKER.

BOSTON.

Published by GEO. P. REED, 17 Tremont Row.

Entered according to Act of Congress in the year 1840 by W.H. Oakes in the Clerks Office of the District Court of Massachusetts.

147. Lithograph music cover, Boston, 1842. *New-York Historical Society.*

148. Lithograph music cover, Baltimore, 1848. *New York, Metropolitan Museum of Art.* ▷

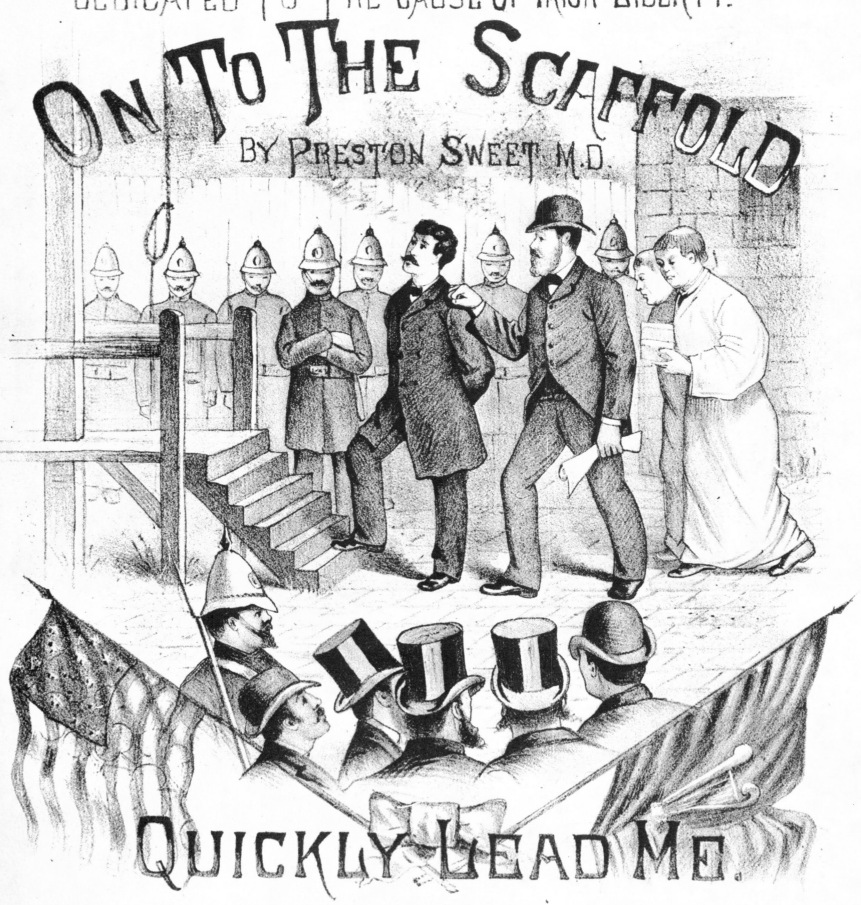

THE FAMOUS
SWEET FAMILY MEDICINES.

DEDICATED TO THE CAUSE OF IRISH LIBERTY.

ON TO THE SCAFFOLD

BY PRESTON SWEET, M.D.

QUICKLY LEAD ME.

WHITE, SMITH & CO.

BOSTON
516 Washington St.

NEW YORK

CHICAGO
5 & 6 Washington St.

SPEAR & DEHNHOFF.
J.L.A. Brodersen & Co. San Francisco.

Copyrighted 1883, by Preston Sweet, M.D.

For sale by all Druggists.

KITTY

150. Engraving by George White, Vermont. *New York, Metropolitan Museum of Art, gift of Mrs. E. C. Chadbourne.*

◁ 149. Lithograph sheet music cover, New York, 1883. *Woodrow Gelman Collection.*

He curvetting and prancing came

151  Grandma knitting socks. Woodcut by the Reverend William Cook in the *Ploughboy, Part I*, Salem, 1851. *New York, Metropolitan Museum of Art.*

152. Woodcut by the Reverend William Cook in the *Ploughboy, Part II*, Salem, 1855. *New York, Metropolitan Museum of Art.*

153. John Randolph of Roanoke, Virginia. Lithograph silhouette by William H. Brown in *Portrait Gallery of distinguished American Citizens,* ▷
Hartford, 1845. *New York, Metropolitan Museum of Art, bequest of Glenn Tilley Morse.*

JOHN RANDOLPH.

From life by Wm.H.Brown.

Lith of E.B.&E.C.Kellogg

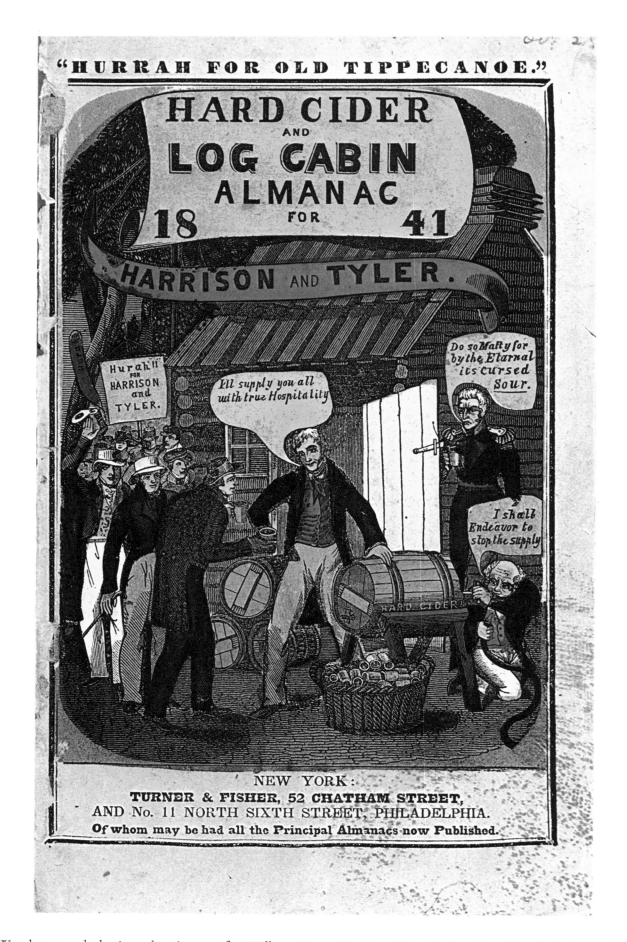

154. Wood-engraved election advertisement for William Henry Harrison, New York, 1841. *New-York Historical Society.*

155. *The Drunkard's Progress, or the Direct Road to Poverty, Wretchedness & Ruin*, New Haven, 1826. *Princeton University Library, gift of Sinclair Hamilton.* ▷

## The CONFIRMED DRUNKARD.

*Beastly Intoxication, Loss of Character, Loss of Natural Affection, Family Suffering, Brutality, Misery, Disease, Mortgages, Sheriffs, Writs &c.*

And lo ! he darts his piercing eye profound,
And looks majestically stern around !

— *The husband and wife, after being sold to different pur-
chasers, violently separated....never to see
each other more.*

156. Thomas Branagan: *Oppression of the Exiled Sons of Africa*, Philadelphia, 1804.
*Princeton University Library, gift of Sinclair Hamilton.*

157. Wood-engraved poster for the American Anti-Slavery Society, New York, 1836. *New-York Historical Society.* ▷

# SLAVE MARKET OF AMERICA.

## THE WORD OF GOD.

"ALL THINGS WHATSOEVER YE WOULD THAT MEN SHOULD DO TO YOU, DO YE EVEN SO TO THEM, FOR THIS IS THE LAW AND THE PROPHETS."

"AND THEY SIGHED BY REASON OF THE BONDAGE, AND THEY CRIED, AND THEIR CRY CAME UP UNTO GOD BY REASON OF THE BONDAGE, AND GOD HEARD THEIR GROANING."

"THUS SAITH THE LORD, EXECUTE JUDGMENT IN THE MORNING, AND DELIVER HIM THAT IS SPOILED OUT OF THE HANDS OF THE OPPRESSOR, LEST MY FURY GO OUT LIKE FIRE, AND BURN THAT NONE CAN QUENCH IT, BECAUSE OF THE EVIL OF YOUR DOINGS."

## THE DECLARATION OF AMERICAN INDEPENDENCE.

"WE HOLD THESE TRUTHS TO BE SELF-EVIDENT;—THAT ALL MEN ARE CREATED EQUAL; THAT THEY ARE ENDOWED BY THEIR CREATOR WITH CERTAIN UNALIENABLE RIGHTS; THAT AMONG THESE ARE LIFE, LIBERTY, AND THE PURSUIT OF HAPPINESS."

## THE CONSITUTION OF THE UNITED STATES.

"THE CITIZENS OF EACH STATE SHALL BE ENTITLED TO ALL THE PRIVILEGES AND IMMUNITIES OF CITIZENS OF THE SEVERAL STATES." ARTICLE 4, SECTION 2.

"CONGRESS SHALL MAKE NO LAW ABRIDGING THE FREEDOM OF SPEECH OR OF THE PRESS, OR OF THE RIGHT OF THE PEOPLE PEACEABLY TO ASSEMBLE, AND TO PETITION THE GOVERNMENT FOR A REDRESS OF GRIEVANCES."—ARTICLE 1, AMENDMENT.

"CONGRESS SHALL HAVE POWER TO EXERCISE EXCLUSIVE LEGISLATION, IN ALL CASES WHATSOEVER, OVER SUCH DISTRICT (NOT EXCEEDING TEN MILES SQUARE) AS MAY, BY CESSION OF PARTICULAR STATES AND THE ACCEPTANCE OF CONGRESS, BECOME THE SEAT OF GOVERNMENT OF THE UNITED STATES."—ARTICLE 1, SECTION 8

## CONSTITUTIONS OF THE STATES.

"EVERY CITIZEN MAY FREELY SPEAK, WRITE, AND PUBLISH HIS SENTIMENTS ON ALL SUBJECTS, BEING RESPONSIBLE FOR THE ABUSE OF THAT LIBERTY." Constitutions of Maine, Connecticut, New-York, Pennsylvania, Delaware, Ohio, Indiana, Illinois, Tennessee, Louisiana, Alabama, Mississippi, and Missouri.

"THE FREEDOM OF THE PRESS IS ONE OF THE GREAT BULWARKS OF LIBERTY, AND THEREFORE OUGHT NEVER TO BE RESTRAINED."—North Carolina.

"THE LIBERTY OF THE PRESS OUGHT TO BE INVIOLABLY PRESERVED."—Maryland.

"THE FREEDOM OF THE PRESS IS ONE OF THE GREAT BULWARKS OF LIBERTY, AND CAN NEVER BE RESTRAINED BUT BY DESPOTIC GOVERNMENTS."—Virginia. Other States nearly the same.

## DISTRICT OF COLUMBIA.

### "THE LAND OF THE FREE."      THE RESIDENCE OF 7000 SLAVES.      "THE HOME OF THE OPPRESSED."

READING OF THE DECLARATION OF INDEPENDENCE.

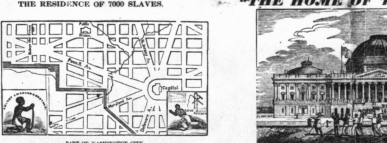

PART OF WASHINGTON CITY.

CAPITOL OF THE UNITED STATES. "HAIL COLUMBIA."

## RIGHT TO INTERFERE.

## PUBLIC PRISONS IN THE DISTRICT.

Built by Congress with $15,000 of the People's money; perverted from the purposes for which they were built, and used by Slaveholders for the confinement of refractory Slaves, by licensed Slave-dealers as depots for their victims, and by kidnappers for the imprisonment of Free Americans, seized and sold to pay their jail fees!

JAIL IN ALEXANDRIA.

### FACTS.

JAIL IN WASHINGTON.—SALE OF A FREE CITIZEN TO PAY HIS JAIL FEES!

### FACTS.

VIEW OF THE INTERIOR OF THE JAIL IN WASHINGTON.—FANNY JACKSON.

### FACTS.

## PRIVATE PRISONS IN THE DISTRICT, LICENSED AS SOURCES OF PUBLIC REVENUE.

"For a license to trade or traffic in slaves for profit, whether as agent or otherwise, four hundred dollars;"—the Register to "deposit all monies received from taxes imposed by this act to the credit of the Canal Fund." Act to provide a revenue for the Canal Fund, approved July 28, 1831. City Laws, p. 249.

SLAVE HOUSE OF J. W. NEAL & CO.

"CASH FOR 200 NEGROES."

JOSEPH W. NEAL & CO.

VIEW OF A SECTION OF ALEXANDRIA, WITH A SLAVE SHIP RECEIVING HER CARGO OF SLAVES.

### "ALEXANDRIA AND NEW-ORLEANS PACKETS."

"Brig TRIBUNE, Captain Smith, and Brig UNCAS, Captain Boush"

FRANKLIN & ARMFIELD.

FRANKLIN & ARMFIELD'S SLAVE PRISON.

"CASH FOR 400 NEGROES."

FRANKLIN & ARMFIELD.

People of the United States, Congress alone possess the constitutional power to legislate for the District of Columbia; yet one hundred and sixty-three of your representatives are striving to perpetuate in the Capital of your Republic this system of robbery, cruelty and despotism. House of Representatives, 8th February 1836.—Certain petitions and resolutions respecting the Abolition of Slavery in the District of Columbia were referred to a Select Committee with instructions to report, "THAT IN THE OPINION OF THIS HOUSE CONGRESS OUGHT NOT IN ANY WAY TO INTERFERE WITH SLAVERY IN THE DISTRICT OF COLUMBIA." Yeas 163—Nays 47.—The following are the Yeas:

Published by the American Anti-Slavery Society, 144 Nassau-street, New-York, 1836.

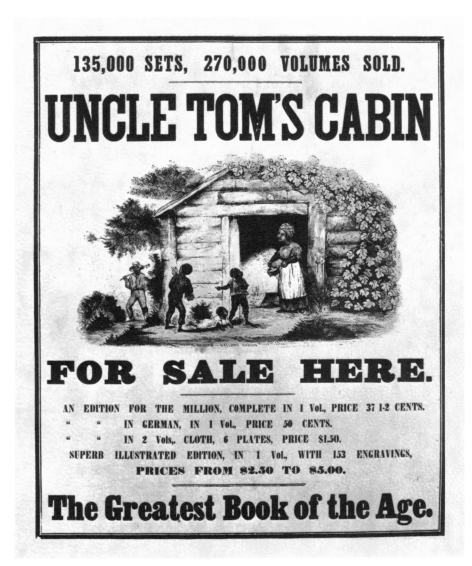

158. Wood-engraved poster, Boston, 1852.
*New-York Historical Society, Bella C. Landauer Collection.*

159. Wood-engraved recruiting poster, Watertown,
Massachusetts, 1861.
*New-York Historical Society.*

160. Wood-engraved election poster, New York, 1860. *New-York Historical Society.* ▷

# UNION NOMINATION

## FOR PRESIDENT,
# Abraham Lincoln
### OF ILLINOIS.

## FOR VICE PRESIDENT,
# Andrew Johnson
### OF TENNESSEE.

JOB PRINTERS, AND ENGRAVERS, LLIAM STREET, NEW DESIGNS FOR ALL POLITICAL P

161. Caricature of Abraham Lincoln.
Etching by Adalbert John Volck in *Confederate War Etchings*, Baltimore, 1864.
*New York, Metropolitan Museum of Art.*

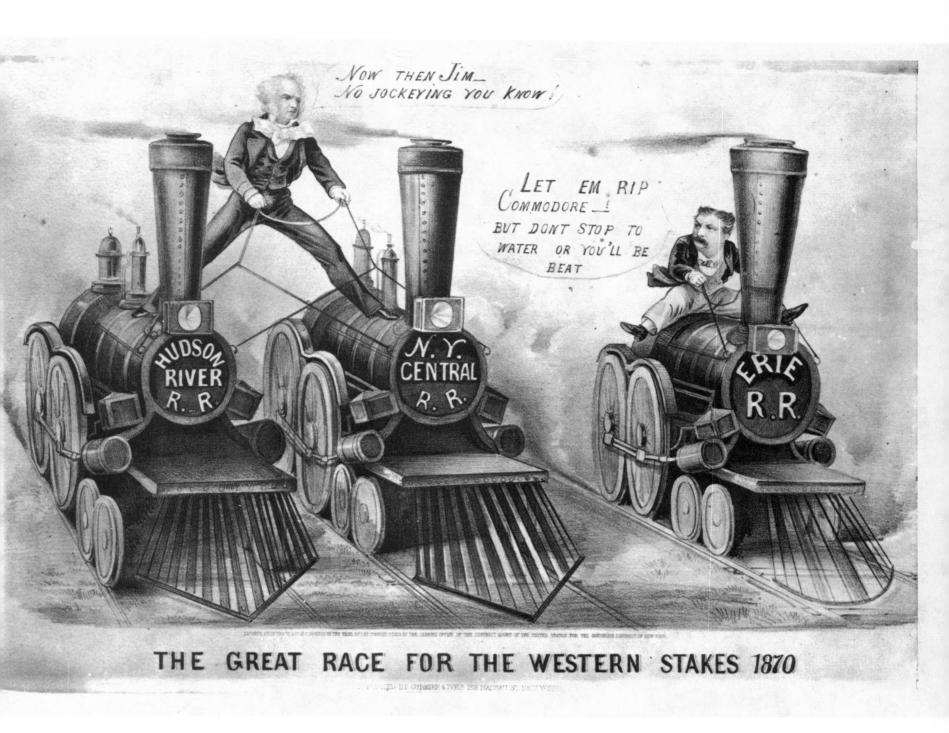

162. Commodore Cornelius Vanderbilt trying to buy the Erie Railroad from Jim Fisk. Lithograph by Currier & Ives, 1870.
*New York, Metropolitan Museum of Art, A. S. Colgate gift.*

Entered according to Act of Congress AD 1865 by Currier & Ives, in the Clerk's Office of the District Court of the United States for the Southern District of New York.

152 NASSAU ST. NEW YORK.

## THE FALL OF RICHMOND, V.ª ON THE NIGHT OF APRIL 2.ᴰ 1865.

This strong hold the Capital City of the Confederacy, was evacuated by the Rebels in consequence of the defeat at "Five Forks" of the Army of Northern Virginia under Lee, and capture of the South side Rail-Road by Gen! Grant.— Before abandoning the City, the Rebels set fire to it, destroying a vast amount of property and the conflagration continued until it was subdued by the Union troops on the following morning.

163. The fall of Richmond, 2 April, 1865. Hand colored lithograph by Currier & Ives, New York, 1865.
*New York, Metropolitan Museum of Art, A. S. Colgate gift.*

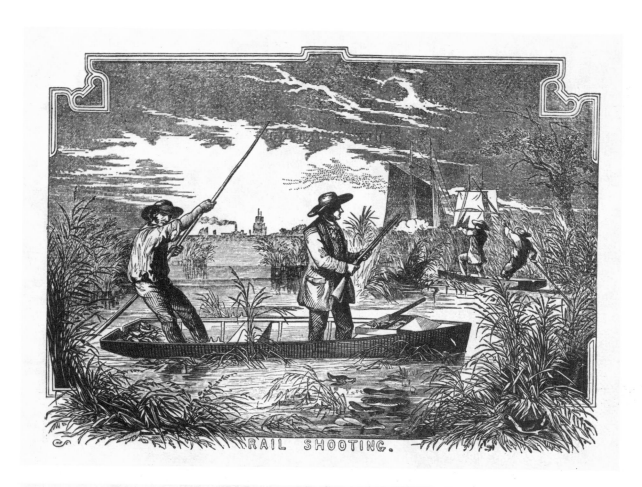

164. Bird-shooting on a marsh at high tide. Wood engraving in *The Sportsman's Portfolio of American Field Sports*, Boston, 1855. *New York Public Library.*

165. Anonymous lithograph, 1850s. *New-York Historical Society.*

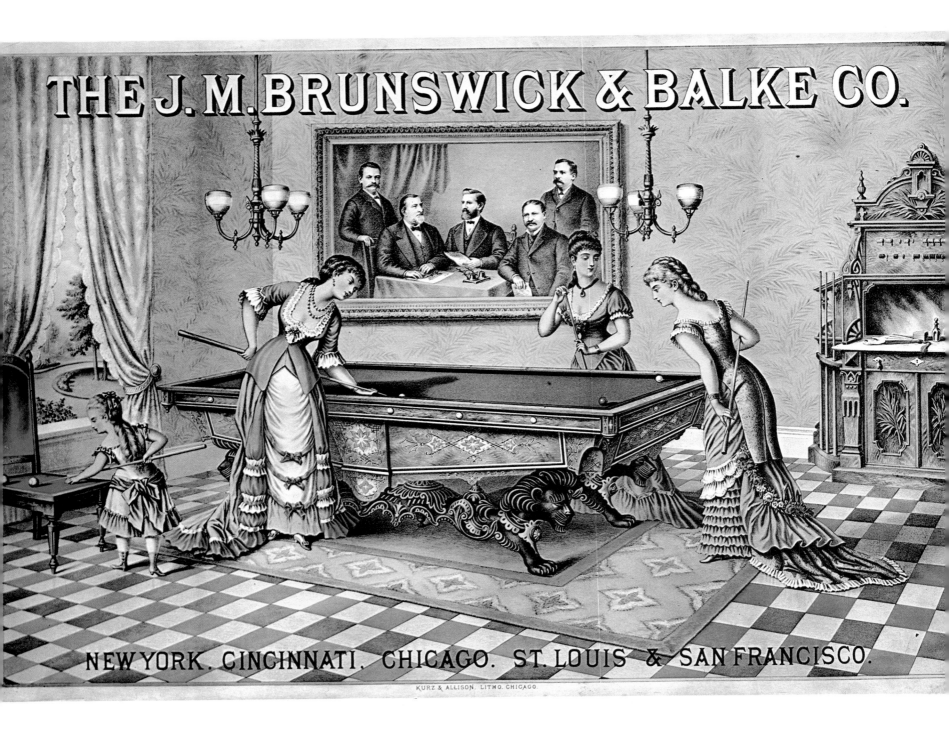

166. Chromolithograph poster, Chicago, 1880s.
*New-York Historical Society, Bella C. Landauer Collection.*

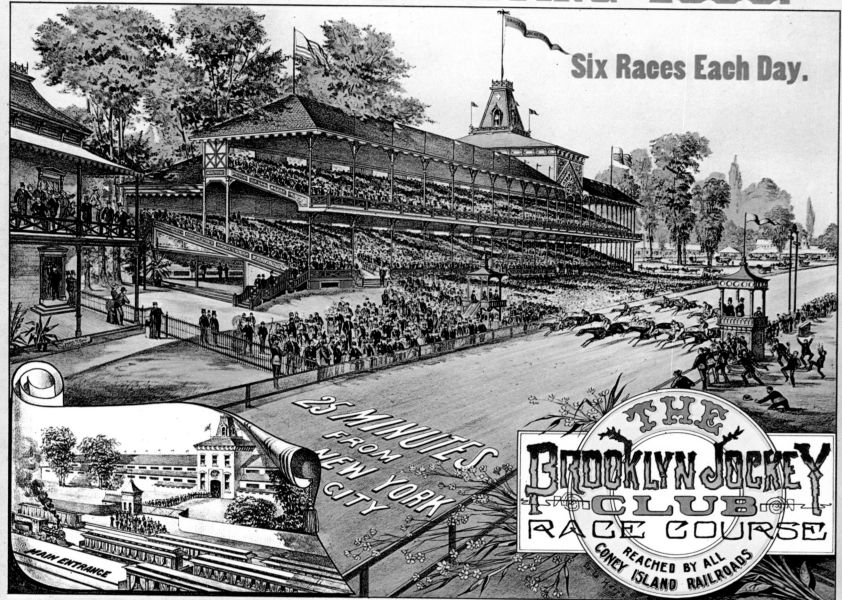

167. Chromolithograph poster, New York, 1886.
*New-York Historical Society, Bella C. Landauer Collection.*

168. Chromolithograph circus poster, New York, 1870s.
*New-York Historical Society, Bella C. Landauer Collection.*

169. Chromolithograph theatrical poster, New York, 1883.
*New-York Historical Society, Bella C. Landauer Collection.*

170. Chromolithograph poster, Currier & Ives, New York, 1890.
*New-York Historical Society, Bella C. Landauer Collection.*

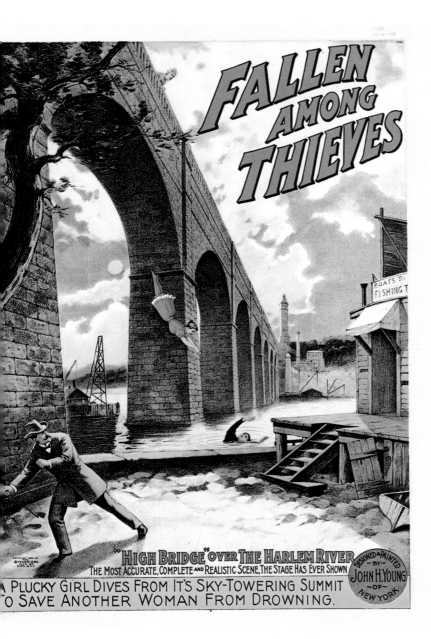

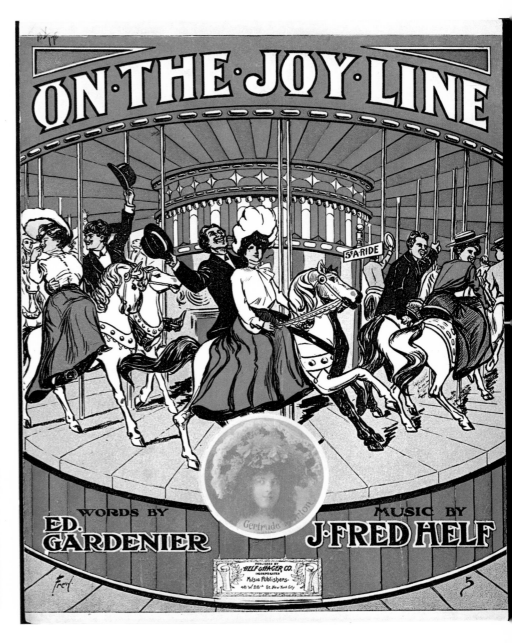

171. Chromolithograph theatrical poster, Cincinnati, 1896.
*New-York Historical Society, Bella C. Landauer Collection.*

172. Music cover, New York, about 1910.
*Woodrow Gelman Collection.*

173. Wood engraved poster, New York, 1859. *New-York Historical Society, Bella C. Landauer Collection.*

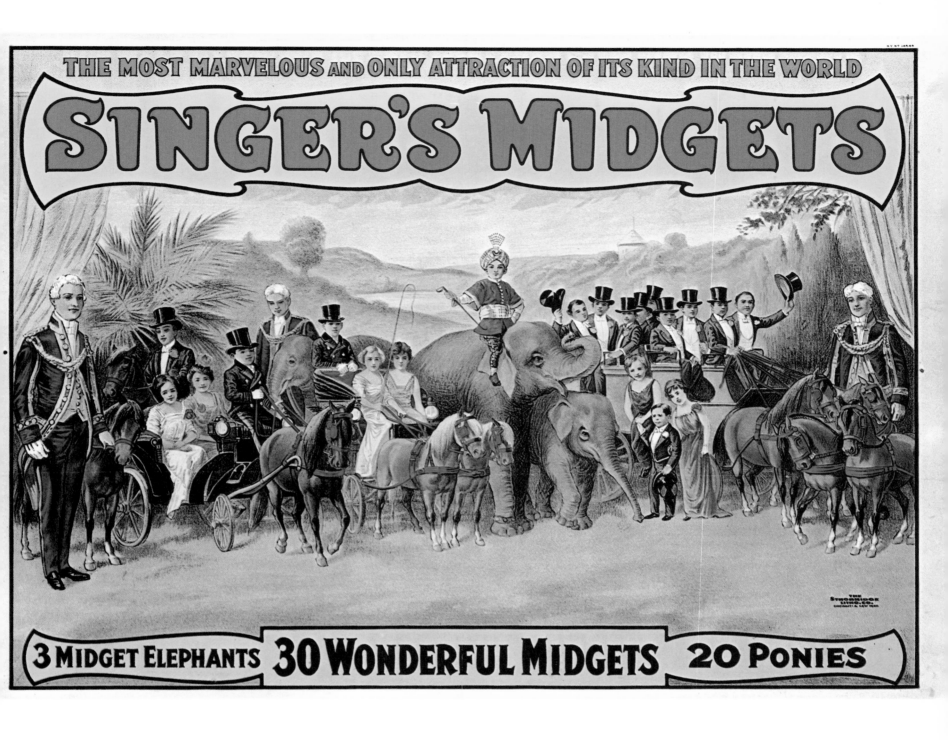

174. Chromolithograph circus poster, Cincinnati, about 1910. *New-York Historical Society, Bella C. Landauer Collection.*

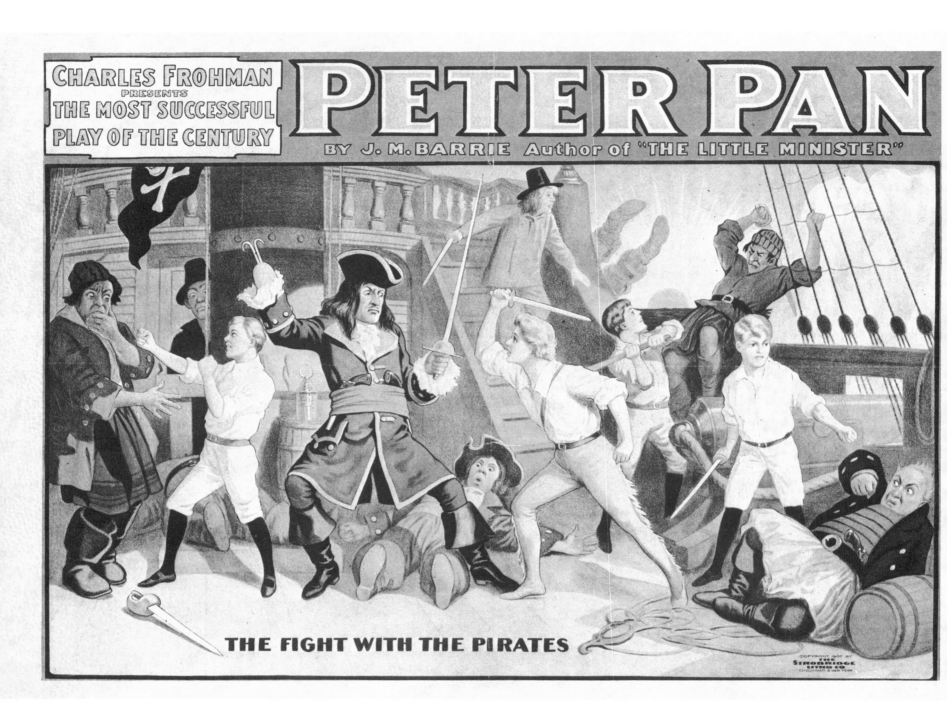

175. Chromolithograph theatrical poster, Cincinnati, 1907. *New-York Historical Society, Bella C. Landauer Collection.*

176. Dime Novel, New York, about 1905. *Woodrow Gelman Collection.* ▷

# THE BUFFALO BILL STORIES

A WEEKLY PUBLICATION

*Devoted to Border History*

Issued Weekly. By Subscription $2.50 per year. Entered as Second Class Matter at New York Post Office by STREET & SMITH, 238 William St., N. Y.

No. 184.                    Price, Five Cents.

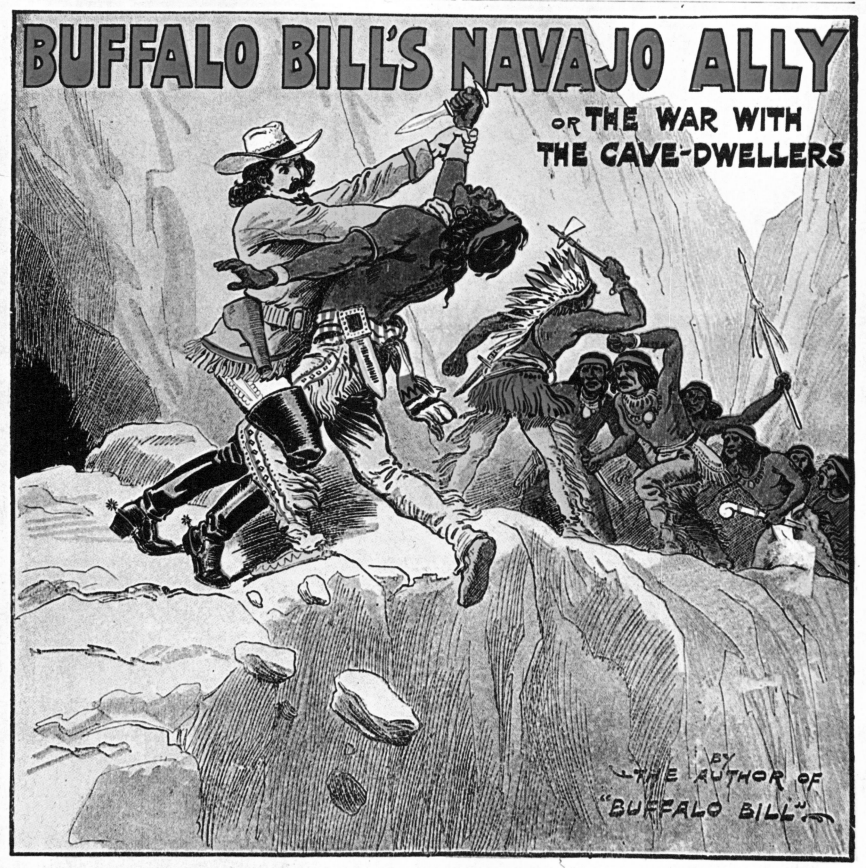

## BUFFALO BILL'S NAVAJO ALLY

### OR THE WAR WITH THE CAVE-DWELLERS

BY THE AUTHOR OF "BUFFALO BILL"

Buffalo Bill and the chief of the Cave-Dwellers struggled on the edge of the precipice, locked in deadly embrace, while the brave Navajo, tomahawk in hand, kept the other Indians at bay.

At the same moment a small, thin hand reached out from somewhere near the waist of the big woman and another gun was held in the hand and pointed at Shadow Steve. "DROP THOSE GUNS," cried Dick Dobbs.

177. Dime Novel, New York, 1909. *Woodrow Gelman Collection.*

178. Dime Novel, New York, 1909. *Woodrow Gelman Collection.* ▷

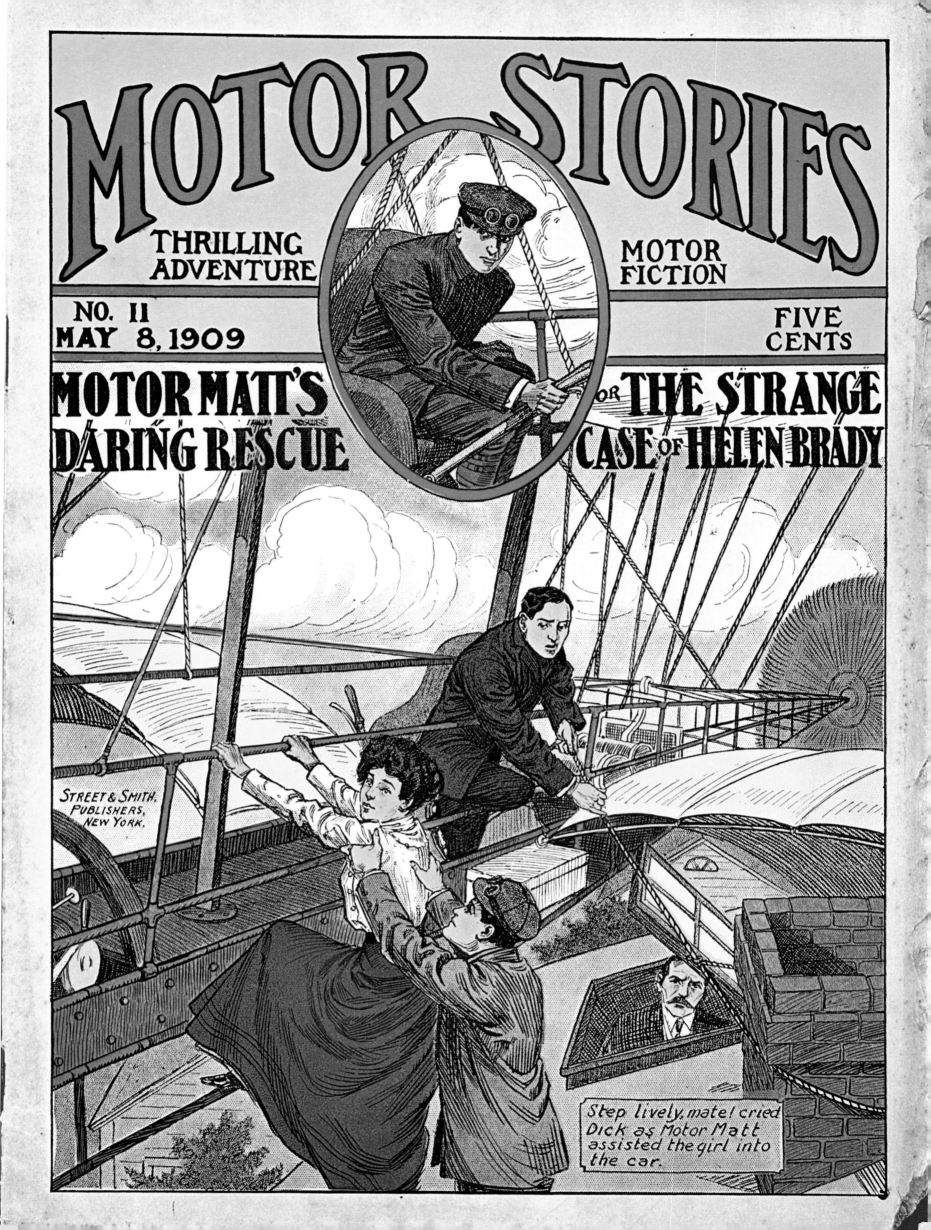

# MOTOR STORIES

### THRILLING ADVENTURE

### MOTOR FICTION

NO. 11
MAY 8, 1909

FIVE CENTS

## MOTOR MATT'S DARING RESCUE

OR THE STRANGE CASE OF HELEN BRADY

STREET & SMITH, PUBLISHERS, NEW YORK.

Step lively, mate! cried Dick as Motor Matt assisted the girl into the car.

179. Dime Novel, New York, 1907. *Woodrow Gelman Collection.*

180. *Police Gazette*, New York, 1899. *Woodrow Gelman Collection.* ▷

MAGNIFICENT DOUBLE SUPPLEMENT NEXT WEEK

# THE NATIONAL POLICE GAZETTE

## THE LEADING ILLUSTRATED SPORTING JOURNAL IN THE WORLD.

Copyrighted for 1899 by the Proprietor, RICHARD K. FOX, The Fox Building, Franklin Square Publishing, Printing and Engraving House, New York City.

RICHARD K. FOX, Editor and Proprietor.

NEW YORK. SATURDAY. APRIL 15. 1899.

VOLUME LXXIV.— No. 1,130
Price 10 Cents.

GAVE HUBBY A WHIPPING.
BECAUSE HE INTERFERED WITH HER AN ACTRESS REPRIMANDS HIM, AT DENVER, COL.

181. Dime Novel, New York, 1904. *Woodrow Gelman Collection.*

182. Magazine Cover, New York, 1913. *Woodrow Gelman Collection.* ▷

# HARPER'S WEEKLY

EDITED by GEORGE HARVEY

John H Coughlin

March 1 1913     HARPER & BROTHERS, N.Y.     Price 10 Cents

# BOWERY BOY
## LIBRARY

Issued Weekly. By Subscription, $2.50 per year. Entered according to Act of Congress in the year 1906, in the office of the Librarian of Congress, Washington, D. C., by THE WINNER LIBRARY CO., 165 West Fifteenth St., New York, N. Y.

**No. 13**      NEW YORK, JANUARY 13, 1906.      **Price, Five Cents**

BOWERY BILLY'S BLAZED TRAIL

OR
THE MAN-HUNTERS OF MANHATTAN.

By
JOHN R. CONWAY
PRIVATE DETECTIVE

With straining muscles and fast-drawn breath, Bowery Billy clung to the sharp-cornered
support while Bludsoe's superb arms pressed him backward.

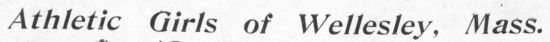

JABBED WITH THE SCISSORS.
PLUCKY INDIANAPOLIS, IND., WOMAN FINDS A CROOK AND GIVES HIM THE WORST OF IT.

184. *Police Gazette*, New York, 1899. *Woodrow Gelman Collection.*

◁ 183. Dime Novel, New York, 1906. *Woodrow Gelman Collection.*

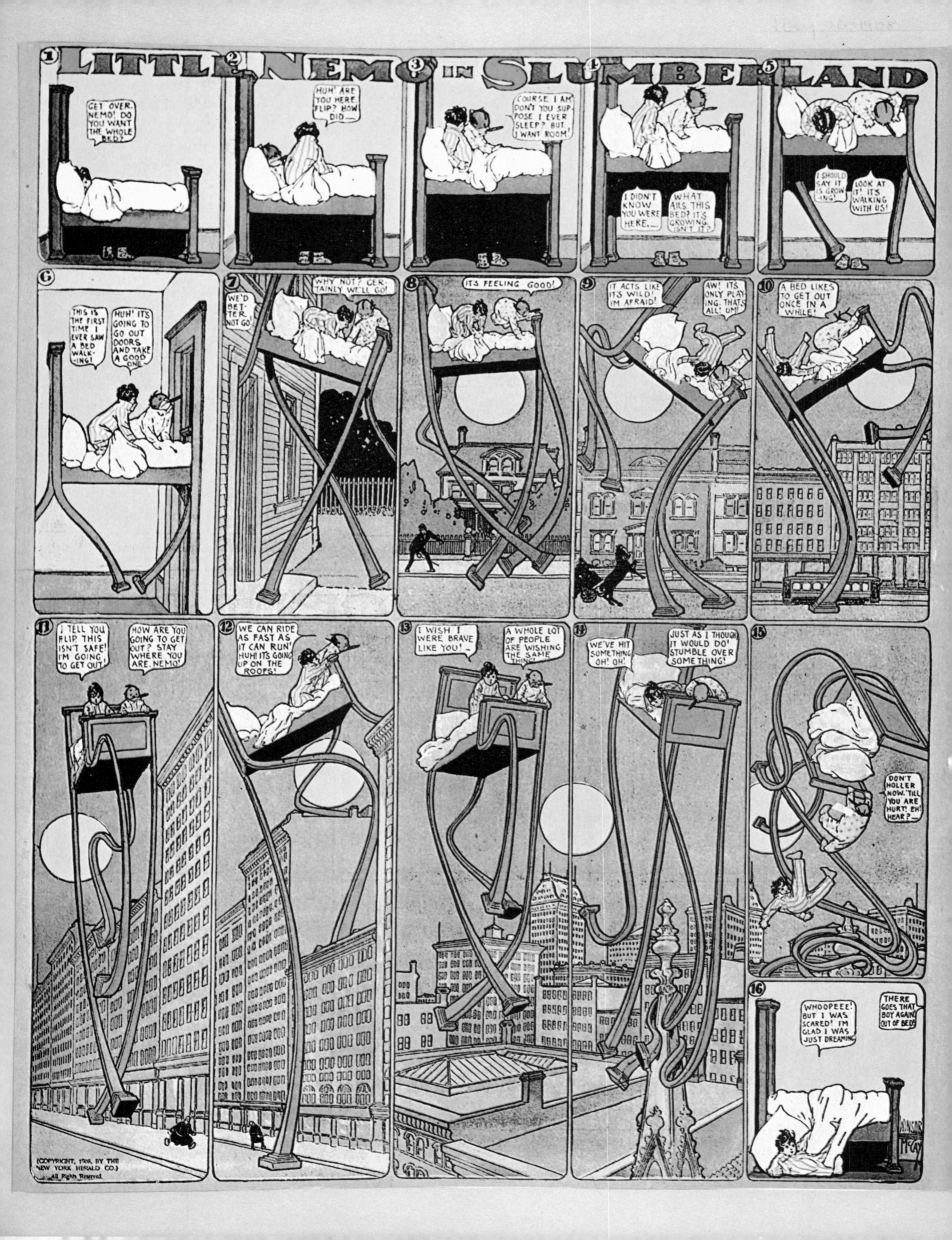

186. Drinking matè in Buenos Aires. Lithograph, Argentina, 1833-34. *New York, Metropolitan Museum of Art.*

◁ 185. *Little Nemo*. Comic Strip by Winsor McCay in the New York Herald, 1905-11. *Woodrow Gelman Collection.*

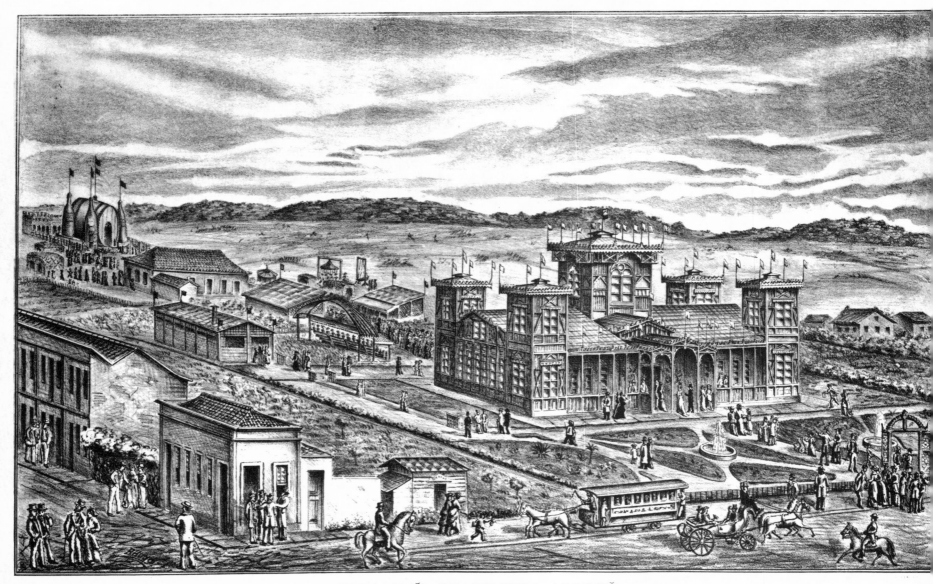

EXPOSIÇÃO BRASILEIRA-ALLEMÃ
PORTO ALEGRE.

187. Lithograph poster for a German trade fair in Brazil, 1870s. *New York, Metropolitan Museum of Art.*

188. Advertisement for a cockfight. Relief etching by Guadalupe Posada. *New York, Metropolitan Museum of Art, Jean Charlot Collection.* ▷

189. The ghost of Pachita the nougat vendor. Relief metal cut by Guadalupe Posada. *New York, Metropolitan Museum of Art, Jean Charlot Collection.*

190. He who was executed. Relief cut by Guadalupe Posada. *New York, Metropolitan Museum of Art, Jean Charlot Collection.*

191. Death of a revolutionary, 1910–12. Relief etching on zinc by Guadalupe Posada. *New York, Metropolitan Museum of Art, Jean Charlot Collection* ▷

# REGALO DE CALAVERAS,

## OBSEQUIO A LAS GARBANCERAS.

# EN PRUEBA DE PURO AMOR
## DISPUTAS DE UN AGUADOR.

Es calavera el inglés,
Calavera el italiano,
Calavera fué el francés
Lo mismo Maximiliano;
El Pontífice romano
Y todos los cardenales,
Reyes, duques, concejales
Y el jefe de la nación
En la tumba son iguales.
Calaveras del montón.

Calavera el general
Y todos sus ayudantes,
Coroneles, comandantes
Y el furioso capitán.
Los subalternos serán
Calaveras en dos tiempos;
En uno son los sargentos,
Los cabos en pelotón,
Los soldados son por cientos
Calaveras del montón.

Toditos los comerciantes
Vendrán á ser calaveras
Porque ahora sí es de deveras
Se acabó la papa de antes;
Calaveras los fabricantes
De labrados y tejidos;
Huesos roídos y podridos
Los dueños de tendajón,
Y todo dueño de giros
Calaveras del montón.

Calavera el dependiente
De cualquier negociación,
De hotel, de fonda ó mesón,
De botica ó de allí enfrente;
Todo el que engaña á la gente
Que vende todo barato;
El baratillero ingrato
Por egoísta y por ahorcón,
Y el del empeño pirata,
Calaveras del montón.

A cuanto mesero veo
Vendiendo velas de cera,
Y todos son calaveras
Que ruedan por el recreo;
Momias secas del museo,
Son toditos los neveros;
Los dulceros, pasteleros,
Y fruteros en unión;
Sean también los mamoneros
Calaveras del montón.

Toditas las chimoleras
Son calaveras en mole,
También las que hacen atole
Juntas con las tamaleras;
Que sigan las tortilleras
Por chorreadas y liendrudas;
Las carniceras sin duda
Por vender mal chicharrón,
Y el que comercia en verdura
Calaveras del montón.

Los ricos por su elegancia,
Los catrines de la media,
Los pobres por su miseria;
Los tontos por su ignorancia,
Los jóvenes por su infancia,
Los hombres de edad madura,
Todos en la sepultura;
Con las viejas ¡¡qué aflicción!!
Serán como dice el cura:
Calaveras del montón.

Calaveras elegantes
Son todos los magistrados,
Los médicos y abogados,
Y también los estudiantes;
También son los practicantes
Del hospital y enfermeros,
Y los Jueces más severos
Que fallan sin compasión,
Que sean con los carceleros
Calaveras del montón.

Los mártires borrachitos
Son ánimas sin pecado,
Pues en el mundo han pagado
Sus penas y sus delitos.
Sufren los inocentitos
Tirándose en duro suelo,
Cuánta aflicción sin consuelo
Si están crudos ó en prisión:
Justo es que vayan al cielo
Sin ser huesos del montón.

Calaveras las mujeres,
Mujeres no más de nombre,
Que les gusta tener hombre
Y no cumplir sus deberes.
Amantes de los placeres,
Que son pocas las honradas
Las más son flacas, son locas
Y pidinches de pilón,
Aunque sean de hábito y toca
Calaveras del montón.

Calaveras infernales
Son las maldecidas viudas,
Traidoras aún peor que Judas
Hipócritas y desleales.
Aparentan sufrir males
Cuando el muerto está tendido,
Pero si han visto al querido
Les dá mal de corazón,
Y dicen es mi marido
Calaveras del montón.

La cocinera chorreada,
La loca recamarera,
La faceta costurera,
La pilmama por arreada;
La corre-chepe malvada
Que trae carta á los amantes,
Carguen con ella los diantres,
Por su mala inclinación,
Y le digan los marchantes
Calavera del montón.

Las pelonas y alisadas
Con manteca relumbrosas
Pezcuezos de hollas sebosas,
Y las que andan muy planchadas.
Las indias patas rajadas
Que ahora usan copete y cola,
Toditas las de la bola
Con las viejas del rincón,
Aquí sí hago carámbola
Calaveras del montón.

Las horribles cacarisas,
Las chatas y las jetonas,
Las altas por tan sanconas,
Las chaparras por erizas,
Las prietas por tan cenizas,
Las blancas por cautelosas,
Las flacas por enredosas
Y las gordas por visión,
Que sean todas horrorosas
Calaveras del montón.

Mas ya se me había olvidado
Enumerar mis parientes
Siendo héroes tan excelentes
Como mi tío el jorobado,
Mi primo el manco me ha dado
Mi pan, mi vela y mi muerto,
Mi sobrino manco y tuerto,
Llora sin consolación,
Porque es en su desacierto
Calavera del montón.

En fin, el compositor
Que versos no supo hacer,
No habrá quién llore por él
Pues antes dirán mejor,
Ya se murió el hablador
Que nos ponía mil defectos,
Que se lo coman los puercos,
Pues no merece panteón
Y que sea entre tantos muertos
Calavera del montón

193. Catrina. Relief etching on zinc by Guadalupe Posada. *New York, Metropolitan Museum of Art, Jean Charlot Collection.*

194. Mexican newspapers represented as *calaveras.* Relief metal engraving by Guadalupe Posada, 1889-95.
*New York, Metropolitan Museum of Art, Jean Charlot Collection.*

◁ 192. Simon the waterseller's wit. Relief metal engraving by Guadalupe Posada. *New York, Metropolitan Museum of Art, Jean Charlot Collection.*

195. Prominent men in the Hoffman House Hotel, New York. Chromolithograph, New York, about 1900. *New-York Historical Society, Bella C. Landauer Collection.*

# BIBLIOGRAPHY

BAIRD, JOSEPH ARMSTRONG. San Francisco: *California Pictorial Letter Sheets*, 1967.

BEEBE, LUCIUS, and CLEGG, CHARLES. New York: *Hear the Train Blow*, 1952.

BELKNAP, WALDRON PHOENIX. Cambridge: *American Colonial Printmaking*, 1959.

BERDECIO, ROBERTO, and APPELBAUM, STANLEY. New York: *Posada's Popular Mexican Prints*, 1972.

BLAND, JANE COOPER. New York: *Currier & Ives, A Manual for Collectors*, 1931.

FIELDING, MANTLE. New York: *American Engravers upon Copper and Steel*, 1917.

GELMAN, WOODROW. New York: *Winsor McCay*, 1973.

GROCE, GEORGE C., and WALLACE, DAVID H. New York: *The New-York Historical Society's Dictionary of Artists in America, 1564–1860*, 1957.

LOPEZ MATEOS, ADOLFO. Mexico: *José Guadalupe Posada, ilustrador de la vida mexicana*, 1963.

OLDS, IRVING S. New York: *The United States Navy*, 1942.
————— New York: *Bits and Pieces of American History*, 1951.

PEARSON, EDMUND. Boston: *Dime Novels*, 1929.

PERRY, GEORGE, and ALDRIDGE, ALAN. New York: *The Penguin Book of Comics*, 1967.

PETERS, HARRY T. New York: *America on Stone*, 1931.
————— New York: *California on Stone*, 1935.
————— New York: *Currier & Ives*, 1929.

*Prints in and of America to 1850*, Winterthur Conference Report, Charlottesville, 1970.

RIVERA, DIEGO, and TOOR, FRANCES. Mexico: *Las obras de José Guadalupe Posada*, 1930.

SHADWELL, WENDY J. New York: *American Printmaking*, 1969.

*Specimens of Poster Cuts* (about 1870) (facsimile). Hollywood: 1968.

STAUFFER, DAVID MCNEELY. New York: *American Engravers upon Copper and Steel*, 1907.

WAINWRIGHT, NICHOLAS B. Philadelphia: *Philadelphia in the Romantic Age of Lithography*, 1958.